Sean Martin

The Pocket Essential

THE BLACK DEATH

www.pocketessentials.com

First published in Great Britain 2001 by Pocket Essentials, 18 Coleswood Road,
Harpenden, Herts, AL5 1EQ

Distributed in the USA by Trafalgar Square Publishing, PO Box 257, Howe Hill
Road, North Pomfret, Vermont 05053

Copyright © Sean Martin 2001
Series Editor: Nick Rennison

A CIP catalogue record for this book is available from the British Library.

ISBN 1-903047-74-9

2 4 6 8 10 9 7 5 3 1

Book typeset by Pdunk
Printed and bound by Cox & Wyman

Acknowledgements

To Steve Skitt, for lending me the Ziegler in the first place; Victoria Carolan, for suggesting I search for the Dols in St Pancras; the Wellcome Trust; the British Library; and the National Centre for Communicable Diseases, for clearing up some issues relating to present-day outbreaks.

As ever, thanks to Nick Rennison, for his reassurances that all will be well (despite my occasional belief otherwise); fellow foot soldier Mike Paine, for the usual reasons; and my sister Lois for her love and wisdom.

This book is heavily indebted to the work of Philip Ziegler, without whom I would have quickly disappeared without trace into the plague pit of history.

Another major source has been Michael W Dols' pioneering study of the effects of the Black Death and its recurrences in the Middle East. His is one of the few books that make it plain that the pandemic was not exclusively a white European affair, and restores to historical visibility the Arab victims and their experience of the plague. What little information there is on the plague in Central Asia has also come from Dols.

CONTENTS

Chapter One: King Death...7

Plagues Before the Black Death, The First Pandemic, The Three Main Types of Plague, Origins of the Black Death, The Black Death Arrives in Europe, Origins of the Name

Chapter Two: Mortal Pestilences and Other Calamities 20

The State of Europe, The Plague Spreads to Italy, The Plague of Florence, the Plague in Other Italian Cities

Chapter Three: Here Death is Chalking Doors with Crosses...37

The Plague in France, Mediaeval Medical Theories, The Plague in Paris and the rest of France

Chapter Four: Satan Triumphant 46

The Plague in Germany, The Flagellants, The Persecution of the Jews

Chapter Five: The Year of the Annihilation................56

The Plague on the Iberian Peninsula, the Plague in North Africa and the Middle East

Chapter Six: The Pestilence Tyme............................64

The Plague in England, Wales, Scotland and Ireland

Chapter Seven: The Triumph of Death.......................77

The Plague in the rest of Europe, The Effects of the Black Death, The Third Pandemic, Latest Research

Selective Chronology of Plague Outbreaks...............86

Suggestions for Further Reading 92

'O Happy posterity, who will not experience such abysmal woe, and will look upon our testimony as a fable.'

- Petrarch

Chapter One: King Death

In early October 1347, twelve Genoese galleys put in at the port of Messina in Sicily. The town was one of the principal stopping off points on the lucrative trade route from the East that brought silks and spices along the Old Silk Road through the Crimea across the Black Sea and into Europe. On this occasion, however, no silks or spices were to be unloaded from the vessels, which had probably come from the trading stations Genoa maintained at Tana and Kaffa on the north coast of the Black Sea. The port authorities found to their horror that scarcely anyone on board the twelve galleys was left alive, and those that were were lethargic with a strange sickness 'that seemed to cling to their very bones'. They suffered from black boils and everything that came out of their bodies – breath, blood, pus – smelled awful. The presence of the galleys was deemed a public health emergency of the first order and, within a day or so, the galleys were driven from the port, so afraid were the Messinese of what they found on board the Genoese vessels. Although the measures were understandably protective, it was too late. The sickness the Genoese crewmen were suffering from took hold of the town within a few days. The doomed galleys drifted on, infecting all who came into contact with them. The Black Death had arrived in Europe.

This was not the first time the plague had struck. The town elders and physicians in Messina may well have known – either from eyewitness reports or from venturing almost certainly suicidally onto the Genoese boats – what the sailors were dying from. There had been outbreaks of plague for generations, usually sporadic, confined to localised areas, lasting a few months, but deadly nonetheless. It had attacked Frederick Barbarossa's army outside Rome in 1167, before it became rife in the city itself, where it recurred in 1230. It had also attacked Florence in 1244, and the south of France and Spain in 1320 and 1333. This time, however, it would be different. This time the plague would not be confined to one or two towns, but would spread unpredictably and, at times it seemed, uncontrollably, across the whole continent, taking rich and poor to their graves in the worst single epidemic in history. But in October 1347, as the Messinese died screaming in their homes and in the streets of what seemed like Divine punishment, the wider world must have been the last thing on their minds.

Plagues before The Black Death

The earliest recorded plagues are those of the Old Testament. Exodus recounts, in chapter 7, how the Lord, displeased with the Pharaoh's detention of the Israelites in Egypt, sent plagues to the land as a punishment. However, it should be noted that the term 'plague' may not necessarily denote plague in its medical sense, and may in fact be simply a generic term for things going rather badly: consider for a moment that the Seven Plagues of Egypt were famously non-bubonic, being successive afflictions of blood, frogs, gnats, flies, the deaths of the Egyptians' animals, boils, hail and locusts rounded off with darkness over the land and the deaths of the first-born.

In 1 Samuel Chapter 5, it is the turn of the Philistines. After capturing the Ark of the Covenant and taking it to the city of Ashdod, they discovered the Lord's displeasure: 'The Lord's hand was heavy upon the people of Ashdod and its vicinity; he brought devastation upon them and afflicted them with tumours.' (Verse 6.) The Septuagint & Vulgate make it clear what this plague is, by adding: 'And rats appeared in their land, and death and destruction were throughout the city.' A few verses later, 'the Lord's hand was against that city, throwing it into a great panic. He afflicted the people of the city, both young and old, with an outbreak of tumours.' Once again, the Septuagint is more explicit, by replacing 'tumours' with 'tumours in the groin.'

That connection between rats and tumours is reinforced in Chapter 6, where, to placate the wrath of the Almighty, the Philistines have to make gold replicas of five rats and five tumours, as there were five Philistine rulers 'because the same plague has struck both you and your rulers'.

Another celebrated outbreak of what could be plague in the medical sense occurred in Athens in the fifth century BC. Thucydides gives a graphic account of the epidemic in his *History of the Peloponnesian War:*

> 'The plague first began to show itself among the Athenians. It was said that it had broken out in many places previously in the vicinity of Lemnos and elsewhere; but a pestilence of such extent and mortality was nowhere remembered. Neither were the physicians at first of any use, ignorant as they were of the proper way to treat it, but they died themselves in great numbers, as they visited the sick most often; nor did any human art succeed any better. Supplications in the temples, divinations, and so forth were found equally futile, till the overwhelming nature of the disaster at last put a stop to them altogether.'

He goes onto describe the symptoms, which included a terrible fever, livid patches on the skin and severe diarrhoea. People were afraid to visit the sick, and the dead were buried without proper funeral rites. So heavy was the mortality that an air of lawlessness began to prevail, with debauchery and crimes proliferating:

'Fear of the gods or the law of man did not restrain them. As for the first, they judged it to be just the same whether they worshipped them or not, as they saw all alike perishing; and for the last, no one expected to live to be brought to trial for his offences, but each felt that a far severer sentence had been already passed upon them all and hung over their heads, and before this fell it was only reasonable to enjoy life a little.'

Whether the Athenian plague really was plague is still a matter for debate, although the symptoms, and the reactions of the Athenians, are remarkably similar to those seen at the time of the Black Death. Eighteen hundred years later, Boccaccio would record the same reactions among the Florentines.

The First Pandemic

The Black Death was the second pandemic of plague. The first is sometimes known as the 'Plague of Justinian', as it occurred during the reign of the Roman Emperor Justinian (527-565). It seems to have come into Egypt at the port of Pelusium in the autumn of 541, from where it travelled west to Alexandria, and from there to the rest of Egypt. It also made its way East into Palestine and Syria: Evagrius Scholasticus, in his *Ecclesiastical History*, describes the plague in his hometown of Antioch in the following year, and says that he believes that the plague originated in Ethiopia. (Thucydides thought the same of the Athenian plague).

Another chronicler of the Plague of Justinian is Procopius, whose *History of the Wars* contains the earliest eyewitness account of plague. He describes how the plague started in Egypt, and spread to the rest of the Byzantine Empire, Europe, Persia and the 'barbarian hinterland'. Egypt and Asia

Minor (modern-day Anatolian Turkey) were particularly badly affected. The plague even reached England, where it was known as the Plague of Cadwallader's Time, before moving on to Ireland and Scandinavia. Byzantium was weakened by the pandemic, and left its frontiers vulnerable to successful resurgences of barbarians: the Balkans and Greece experienced Slavic migrations, the Lombards invaded Italy while the Berbers made inroads into Byzantine North Africa.

Unlike the Black Death, the Justinian plague probably came from East Africa. The Byzantine historian Theophylact Simocattes (who continued Procopius's *History* for the Emperor Maurice) writes that an embassy of Turks visited the Emperor in 598, and told him that in Mogholistan (near lake Issyk-Kul in modern day Kyrgyzstan) they had not experienced contagious disease since the times of the ancients, and that earthquakes were rare. This would seem to rule out an Asian transmission for the first pandemic, and confirm the belief shared by Evagrius and the Arab doctor Ali ibn Rabban at-Tabari, who wrote a medical compendium in the ninth century, that the Justinian plague travelled North along the trade routes from Ethiopia and the Sudan. Ironically, although Issyk-Kul escaped the first pandemic, it would be one of the first places to be affected in the second pandemic, that of the Black Death.

The Three Main Types of Plague

The Black Death has traditionally been seen as a mixture of bubonic, septicaemic and pneumonic plague. Current research suggests that another, unknown, factor may have also been at work, making the Black Death particularly virulent. Plague is endemic to a number of regions of the world, including Africa and Central Asia, which were the cradles of all three pandemics (the third starting in China in the mid nineteenth century). The peoples of Transbaikalia and Outer Mongolia knew of plague, and it was also known in Tibet. It is possibly also endemic in Europe, but on a vastly lesser level.

The plague bacillus, *yersinia pestis*, lives in the bloodstream of small rodents such as rats, squirrels or mice. When a flea, usually the rodent's familiar, *xenopsylla cheopsis*, feeds on an infected host, the plague bacillus will multiply inside the flea's body, blocking its oesophagus and making it thirsty. When the rodent it has been feeding on dies, it will look for another host to drink from, and, in doing so, will pass the bacillus into the new host's blood stream as it drinks.

Plague attacks the lymphatic system, and produces boils or buboes in the groin, armpits and neck. (Bubo is from the Greek *boubon*, meaning groin.) The buboes can vary in size, from that of an almond to an orange, and are extremely painful. Usually the victim will only develop one; if more develop they will usually be on the same chain of lymph glands. If the buboes suppurate within a week, the victim will usually recover. If not, as happened in the majority of cases, the victim will die.

Although buboes are the most well-known symptom of plague, the victim will also develop blotches on the skin, caused by subcutaneous haemorrhages, fever, vomiting, extreme headaches, giddiness, intolerance to light, pains in the abdomen, back and limbs, sleeplessness, diarrhoea, apathy and delirium. This is bubonic plague.

Pneumonic, or pulmonary, plague occurs when the plague victim develops pneumonia. It attacks the lungs and its most obvious symptom is the coughing up of blood. It is also more infectious than bubonic plague, as, every time the victim coughs, they will expel plague bacilli as well as blood, causing airborne transmission. The victim will also be feverish, as with bubonic plague, and will experience difficult and rapid breathing. Whereas with bubonic, there is some chance of survival if the buboes suppurate, the mortality rate for pneumonic plague is almost 100%.

Septicaemic plague occurs when the bacillus cannot locate in the lymphatic system, and instead affects the bloodstream. The bacillus will multiply profusely, causing the blood to become so quickly and totally infected that it can be transmitted by the human flea, *pulex irritans*. (Normally the human flea would not be able to drink enough blood to be able to transmit a fatal dose. By the time the bloodstream would become infected enough for a flea to be able to do so, the victim would be dead and buried. Or if not buried, then piled up in the street awaiting burial in the common pit, and fleas do not feed on corpses.) Although the rarest form of the main three types of plague, septicaemic is perhaps the most frightening. There are no visible symptoms other than sudden death; buboes do not even have time to form. Stories of people going to bed seeming well in the evening and being found dead in bed the next morning would seem to be the work of the plague is its septicaemic form.

Why endemic diseases such as plague become epidemics and pandemics is still a matter for research. Usually, a variety of factors will cause the host to leave its native habitat and seek new territories. In the case of the Black Death, those factors seemed to have occurred in the years immediately before 1347. In abundance.

The Origins of the Black Death

The Arab historian Ibn al-Wardi, who witnessed the Black Death at Aleppo and died of it himself in 1349, believed that the pestilence had originated some fifteen years earlier in the 'land of darkness', by which he probably meant Mongolia. If this were the case, then it would mean that the plague was raging in Central Asia in the early 1330s. Another Arab writer, Al-Maqrizi, described the plague as striking an area that lay six months' journey from Tabriz; again, this could well mean Mongolia or Northern China. He writes that 300 tribes were wiped out, including 16 princes who all succumbed within 3 months of each other.

Although Al-Maqrizi's chronicle was not contemporaneous, Chinese records from the period provide information that may corroborate his thesis that the plague was raging in Mongolia in the early 1330s. The Great Mongol Khan Jijaghatu Toq-Temür died on 2 October 1332, aged 28, and his sons followed him in rapid succession. The Khan's predecessor, Yesün Temur, had also died suddenly of an unknown illness on 15 August 1328. If he was a victim of plague, then he would be the Black Death's earliest recorded victim.

The Chinese chronicles report these deaths amid repeated stories of natural disasters and cataclysms that were afflicting China at the time with alarming – one might be tempted to say almost Old Testament - frequency. In 1333, famine followed the drought that had parched the area between the Kiang and Hoai Rivers. Following the drought, there was a deluge; 400,000 are said to have died. Tsincheou Mountain partially collapsed, causing huge faults to appear in the landscape. The following year, 1334, was no better. Houkouang and Honan provinces experienced drought, followed by a famine attended by clouds of locust. An earthquake in the Ki-Ming-Chan Mountains brought floods that were so bad they created a new lake and in Tche the dead were said to amount to more than five million. If this wasn't bad enough, the earthquakes that had presumably caused Mount Tsincheou to cave in continued up until 1345, along with further floods and crop-destroying locusts.

Amidst all this chaos, humans would not have been the only occupants of China and Mongolia to have become virtual refugees in their own land. The lives of the rodent population would have been equally disrupted. It is probably this series of disasters that forced them to migrate, taking with them the plague bacillus. They must have headed south, taking the plague to India, and west, where the plague seems to have reached Lake Issyk-Kul by the end of the decade. Nestorian gravestones on the shores of the lake memorialise huge numbers of people who died in 1338 and 1339. The stones attribute the deaths to plague.

From here, the plague would have been taken further West by the caravans that plied a regular trade between China and the East and the trading stations of the Crimea, which were owned by the Genoans and Venetians. Genghis Khan had established the Eastern end of the route as early as 1219, and further Mongol conquests had made China, Turkestan, Persia and Southern Russia one empire and therefore safe to all merchants. By the middle of the fourteenth century, the route was secure and busy. The plague carrying fleas easily made the jump from rats and marmots to making a new home in the cloths, rugs and furs bound for Europe and the markets of the Middle East. The plague seems to have moved slowly, however, no doubt seeping south and infecting cities such as Samarkand and Tashkent at the same time as it made a leisurely progress westward, where it reached Sarai on the banks of the Volga in 1345. Sarai was a cosmopolitan city, capital of the Golden Horde, the region of modern Ukraine that had been conquered by Genghis Khan's grandson between 1236 and 1239.

During 1346, the plague spread south to Astrakhan and into Azerbaijan. More disastrously, it spread further West into the Crimea, an area important to both Christian and Muslim traders. 85,000 people were said to have died in the Crimea that year, and Muslim traders decided that the Christian merchants must somehow be responsible for the appalling mortality. They attacked the Genoese trading station at Tana, forcing the Christians to retreat to their coastal station at Kaffa, on the Northern shore of the Black Sea. The Kipchak Khan Janibeg took charge of the siege, and instructed his men to bombard the Genoese into submission. The Tartar army's strength was seriously weakened by the appearance of plague in its ranks, and the whole campaign was almost called off. Janibeg decided that the Genoese should also suffer the plague, and had the bodies of its victims catapulted over the walls of Kaffa. In the confined environment of a walled city, the plague quickly did its work. No matter how fast the Genoese merchants disposed of the bodies of the Khan's troops by dumping them in the Black Sea, they couldn't outrun the pace of the disease. They took to their boats and fled. Within a few days, they would have realised that they had unwittingly brought the plague with them.

The Byzantine historian Nicephoros Gregoras described the plague's progress to the West of the Bosphorous. After ravaging Constantinople (where Nicephoros witnessed it at first hand), the disease travelled south, bifurcating in the Mediterranean and heading simultaneously towards Europe and also toward the Middle East, depending upon which port the merchants were bound for. If the ships had no cloth aboard, the plague-carrying fleas would have easily found a home in the fur of the ships' rats. Every ship became a potential carrier of the plague, and it was twelve of those vessels travelling from the Crimea that brought the Black Death to Sicily in October 1347.

The Black Death Arrives in Europe

Despite the fact that the authorities in Messina had driven the plague infested vessels from the port, they were too late to stop the disease taking hold of the town within a matter of days. The Messinese who were able fled to Catania, the next town, where they were at first admitted to hospital. Only when the new arrivals started to infect the rest of their patients, did the Catanians imposed a strict quarantine on anyone coming into the town. Immigrants from Messina – or from anywhere else for that matter – who died of plague were to be buried in a pit outside the city walls. But it was no use. Soon hundreds were dying in Catania too.

After the apparent failure of quarantine to halt the progress of the disease, appeal was made to the Archbishop of Catania. Perhaps if the relics of St Agatha could be processed from Catania to the source of all the trouble, Messina, then all their suffering might be alleviated? It was only a protest from the able-bodied Catanians that stopped the Archbishop. They felt that perhaps St Agatha would be best left in her own cathedral, where prayers to her might have more effect. In the end, the Archbishop dipped the relics in water and took that to Messina instead.

During a further procession returning to Messina with an icon of the Virgin borrowed from a nearby shrine, a bad omen occurred: the horse carrying the image refused to enter the city. Although it was eventually made to continue on to its destination of the church of Santa Maria la Nuova, it was seen as the Mother of God herself deserting the Messinese.

Michael of Piazza, a Franciscan friar who wrote one of the earliest European accounts of the plague in the 1350s, writes that the Messinese begged the Virgin not to punish them for their sins.

One of the earliest plague chronicles, aside from Michael's, is by Gabriel de Mussis, who was originally thought to have been on one of the galleys that brought the plague to Europe (it later transpired that he sat out the epidemic in his home town of Piacenza). De Mussis makes it plain that people thought the plague had been sent as a punishment from God for their sins. In de Mussis' account, God sees 'the entire human race wallowing in the mire of manifold wickedness.' God then pronounces judgment on humanity: 'May your joys be turned to mourning, your prosperity be shaken by adversity, the course of your life be passed in never-ending terror. Behold the image of death. Behold I open the infernal floodgates... Let the sharp arrows of sudden death have dominion throughout the world. Let no one be spared.... Let the innocent perish with the guilty and no one escape.'

Anything unusual or portentous, such as the horse refusing to carry on into Messina, particularly heavy rainfalls or the birth of Siamese twins, were seen as proof that God had abandoned his people. This despondency, evident in Sicily, and the feeling that plague was the wrath of God, would accompany the Black Death as it made its inexorable way into Italy, and mainland Europe.

The Origins of the Name

When Michael wrote his chronicle, he did not refer to the plague as the Black Death. This name, traditionally thought to refer to the buboes that the victims would develop, in fact does not seem to have been used until 1555, when a Swedish chronicle employs the term. In the early seventeenth century, it appears in a Danish work, and in Britain it began to be used after 1665, when it was used to distinguish it from the Great Plague of 1665. It does not appear to have gained widespread use to refer to the pandemic of the 1340s until the 18th century.

Black Death is usually taken to have been a mistranslation into either English or Swedish of the Latin *atra mors*, or *pestis atra*. The word *atra* can mean *terrible* or *dreadful* as well as *black*.

Contemporaneous references from Europe usually designate the Black Death as the 'great pestilence', 'the mortality', 'the pestilence tyme', 'the plague of Florence' or simply as 'the plague'. Their Arabic counterparts were somewhat more imaginative in the choice of words: Muslim chronicles refer to it as 'the universal plague', 'the great destruction' and 'the year of the annihilation.'

Chapter Two: Mortal Pestilences and Other Calamities

The Europe that the Black Death ravaged had been experiencing a period of sustained economic growth that began in the 12th century. The Crusades, in focusing the attention of Christendom on the retaking of Jerusalem and the establishing of permanent Christian settlements in the Holy Land - in addition to removing troublesome elements who fancied their chances of wealth, glory and a good scrap in the Middle East - had helped to usher in an extended period of peace in Europe that greatly contributed to increasing levels of prosperity and security. That is not to say that the continent as a whole was suddenly experiencing paradisiacal conditions, but compared to what it had been through in the preceding centuries, those of the European Dark Ages, it was certainly a greatly less worse place in which to live.

The improving situation in Europe, while obviously not affecting every single member of the population, was nevertheless spread across almost every band of the social spectrum. Land values increased; rent did not. In the Rhine and Moselle valleys, land was worth seventeen times as much at the end of the thirteenth century as it had been at the beginning of the tenth. More land was under till in 1300 than ever before, and would not be matched again until 1800, when Europe was once again undergoing a period of massive change, that of the Industrial Revolution.

In the world of learning, there was similar growth, which has been called the Renaissance of the Twelfth Century. Cities were expanding, and Europe's economy was slowly becoming both urbanized and rationalized. Advances were made in many walks of life: in navigation, animal husbandry and Fibonacci's new method of double-entry bookkeeping. Official learning was dominated by the University of Paris, where logicians such as Peter Lombard and the still only partially translated works of Aristotle dominated the intellectual climate. Other advances made in Paris were in the sphere of music: plainchant was gradually giving way to the first four part polyphony in the shape of the works of Perotin. The work of Arab scholars such as Avicenna and Averroes were being translated for the first time into Latin – largely in the Iberian translation schools such as Cordoba, whose Arab-friendly climate was the opposite of the staunchly conservative Parisian scene. A further influence of Arabic thought would be felt in the sphere of architecture, in the shape of the arrival of Gothic churches in the mid-twelfth century. The style was enthusiastically embraced across Europe, with Chartres just outside Paris being perhaps the most celebrated example. It was not widely known at the time that the style derives from principles imported into Europe by the Templars, who were known for their heretical friendliness with Arab scholars.

One major factor in Europe's growth was demographic. There were simply more Europeans than ever before. The population had been growing relentlessly until, by the middle of the thirteenth century, Europe was starting to suffer from overcrowding. Certain areas would not witness similar levels of overpopulation until the late nineteenth and start of the twentieth centuries. In Pistoia in Tuscany, the density of population was 38 per square kilometre, a level which would not be reached again for five hundred years. In Oisans, near Grenoble, the population stood at 13,000 in 1339, which was only bettered by the 13,805 recorded in 1911. Towns grew to support populations of ten or twenty thousand; the number of bourgeoning cities on the map continued to increase.

The growth was starting to slow down by the end of the thirteenth century. Indeed, signs of crisis were looming. The growth of towns and cities meant that the economy would start to become more urbanized and industrialized, with demand starting to outstrip supply. Intensive farming had led to poor soil in many areas after the failure to let land lie fallow. There were famines in England in 1272, 1277, 1283, 1292 and 1311, and the weather exacerbated the situation. There were bad harvests across Europe between 1315 and 1319. The lack of sun hindered the production of salt, making the preservation of what meat there was even more difficult. In England, the wheat doubled in price, forcing the poor to eat dogs, cats, manure and even their own children. At Ypres, ten per cent of the population died of starvation. Even before Europe had time to recover, disaster struck again: 1332 brought further crop failures, recurring yet again between 1345 and 1348.

By the time the Black Death appeared, Europe was in recession. The cloth trade had stagnated, agricultural prices fell; what had once been the surest indicators of Europe's untrammelled growth were now showing that things were slowing down, almost to a halt. Malnutrition was more widespread than at any time for generations, and with the effective end of the Crusades, political tensions within Europe were once again causing fissures to appear. In this depressed, divided continent, the Black Death found easy pickings.

The Plague Spreads to Italy

The Black Death's arrival in mainland Italy in January 1348 was, it seemed to many at the time, to be God's wrath upon a faithless and sinful people. 'The scale of the mortality', wrote de Mussis, 'and the form which it took persuaded those who lived, weeping and lamenting, through [those] bitter events... that the last judgment had come.' This was not entirely the product of Church indoctrination; the Italians had suffered a litany of catastrophes in the years immediately before the arrival of the plague that could stand comparison with those experienced by the Chinese. When the plague struck, Rome, Pisa, Bologna, Padua, Venice and Naples were still in the process of recovering from recent earthquakes. 1345 had seen almost six months of continuous rain, making sowing almost impossible in many areas; the corn crop was a quarter of its usual yield.

Even the richest cities and states were not immune, with food shortages in 1346 and 1347 reducing some to eating grass and weeds. Prices soared, with the cost of wheat doubling during the early months of 1347. By Easter, bread was being rationed to 94,000 people in Florence alone, where prosecutions for all minor debts were suspended and all but the most serious felons released from jail. 4,000 Florentines died of malnutrition. The city was also beset with financial difficulties. The great banking house of Peruzzi had been declared bankrupt in 1343, with the Acciaiuolis and the Bardis joining them in liquidation in 1345. By 1346, Florentine bankers had lost 1.7 million florins, and almost every house was in difficulty.

Needless to say, Italy's famously fractious political arena was experiencing one of its more combustible periods, with fighting between the Guelphs and the Ghibellines; meanwhile, the Orsini were scrapping with the Colonna; Genoa and Venice, the first two mainland city states to feel the brunt of the Black Death, were at each other's throats; while the Visconti picked quarrels seemingly at random. German freebooters were taking pickings wherever they could, and Lewis of Hungary's men were marching on Naples in retaliation for Queen Joanna's murder of Lewis's brother. Rome had not recovered from the loss of the Papacy to Avignon, and there was a general sense of malaise. All greatness seemed to have departed Italy along with the Pope, leaving seemingly endless and potentially fatal internecine quarrels to fill the political stage.

When boats bearing the Black Death put it at Genoa and Venice at the start of 1348, the pattern that was established at Messina repeated itself. By the time the ships were identified as bearing the plague, it was too late. The ships were repelled from the harbours with burning arrows and whatever siege engines were available to lob projectiles at them. The ships took to the seas and, in the case of the ships from Genoa, sailed west, where they sought sanctuary in French ports, and thus spread the disease rapidly along the coast of the South of France towards the Iberian peninsula and the Balearics.

The Plague of Florence

Pisa was attacked in February, which seems to have been the Black Death's main entry point into Northern Italy. Rome was infected, and also the beleaguered Florence. The plague struck Florence with such exceptional ferocity that it is sometimes known not as the Black Death, but as the Plague of Florence. The reasons for this are twofold: Florence was the first major city to be seriously affected, and it was immortalised in Giovanni Boccaccio's *The Decameron*.

In *The Decameron*, Boccaccio has a group of wealthy Florentines fleeing to the hills and entertaining themselves with stories while the plague rages outside their isolated villa. The introduction is perhaps the most celebrated description of the Black Death:

'I cannot hide from myself that this work has a heavy and distressing prelude, in that it will revive the memory of the recent mortal pestilence, whose terrible force was evident not only to eyewitnesses but to anyone who had knowledge of it in anyway.

'In the year 1348, the deadly pestilence appeared in the illustrious city of Florence, the fairest of all Italian cities. Whether it was disseminated by the influence of the planets, or sent by God in His wrath for our iniquities, it had had its origin some years earlier in the East, when, after killing innumerable people, it had spread without mercy from place to place, and, ultimately, to the West.

'In Florence, despite all that could be done to avert it, such as cleaning the streets, refusing to admit sick travellers, and adopting many other precautions; despite also prayers addressed to God, frequently repeated both in public processions and in private; despite this, towards the beginning of spring the doleful effects of the pestilence began to be horribly apparent.

'The symptoms were not like those in the East, where bleeding from the nose was a sure sign of impending death; but in both men and women the pestilence first betrayed itself by the emergence of tumours in the groin or in the armpits, some of which grew as large as an apple, or an egg. From these two parts of the body the tumours soon began to spread themselves in all directions; black or livid spots of varying sizes appeared after this on the arm or the thigh or even around the waist. Like the tumours, these spots were also seen as a sign of approaching death. Doctors could do nothing. Whether they were at fault or whether the disease was untreatable, I do not know. To make things worse, men and of women, none of whom were qualified in medicine, tried to treat people as well. Hardly anyone survived. Almost all died within three days from the appearance of the tumours, in most cases without any fever or other symptom.

'What's more, the virulence of the disease was increased through merely talking to the sick, just as fire burns things that are brought close to it. And if that wasn't bad enough, it was possible to become infected even by touching the clothes of the sick or anything else that they had touched or used. Once I saw two pigs in the street come up to the clothes of a poor man. He had died of the disease and his things were scattered outside his house. The pigs took the garments between their teeth and chewed them. Almost immediately, they fell down dead, as if poisoned. Had I not seen this with my own eyes, I would have hardly dared believe it, much less set it down in writing.

'In these circumstances, people began to shun all contact with the sick, and vowed to stay as healthy as possible. Some thought that to live temperately and avoid all excess would be best. Small groups of people banded together, and lived in isolation. They exercised the utmost care, avoiding every kind of luxury, and ate and drank in moderation. They spoke to no one, in case they should hear about sickness or death, and kept themselves busy with music and discussions and games.

'Other people thought that debauchery was the answer, and resorted day and night to taverns, drinking with total disregard for everything, or visiting other peoples' houses if they saw anything in them that they liked, which wasn't too difficult, as their owners, expecting to die at any moment, had become as reckless as their guests, and threw their houses open to all comers. In this extremity of suffering all laws, both human and divine, were ignored for lack of people to uphold them as they were either dead or sick, and everyone was free to do whatever they wanted.

'Some people steered a middle course, neither being wary of their health nor living a life of dissipation. They walked around carrying flowers or fragrant herbs, which they held to their noses, thinking that it would provide some comfort against the air which reeked with the stench of the dead and dying.

'Yet others, the most sound of judgement, perhaps, felt that the best medicine was to flee; a multitude of men and women deserted the city, their houses, their estates, their families, their goods, and went into voluntary exile, fled to the country, hoping that God would not pursue them with His wrath, but would only destroy those who stayed behind.

'Whatever course of action people took, many died. Citizen avoided citizen, neighbours lost all feeling for each other, families met only rarely; so afraid were people of this disease, that brother forsook brother, nephew uncle, brother sister, and often husbands their wives; what's more, scarcely believable, is that parents abandoned their children, and left them to their fate, as if they had belonged to strangers. The huge numbers of sick had no choice but to rely on the charity of what few friends they had left, or servants, who demanded high wages for their care, (despite not being qualified) and who merely looked after the immediate wants of the sick, and watched them die; they very often died too. There were so few people left to care for the sick that no woman, however fair or well-born she might be, shrank, when stricken with the disease, from the ministrations of a man, and willingly exposed to him every part of her body; some received the man's physical attention rather than medical aid. Possibly, with better care, some may have survived, but the combination of so virulent a plague and such poor medical aid resulted in huge mortality, with deaths taking place day and night; those who witnessed it – or even heard about it second hand - were struck dumb with amazement.

'Traditionally, during a funeral, the women would gather inside the house and wail their laments, while the men would gather outside with the priest to carry the body to the church requested by the deceased in their will. However, with the pestilence raging so furiously, these arrangements were soon dropped. Most died without a crowd of mourning women; most would-be mourners were either dead or out getting drunk, which was good for the health of the women, who did not have to go near a corpse or mix with others. Most biers were not carried by friends and neighbours, but by the desperate becchini, who hired themselves out for such awful tasks, and would carry the body, not to the church of the deceased's choice, but to whichever one was nearest to hand, with four or six priests in front carrying possibly a candle or two; nor did the priests bother to conduct too long and solemn a funeral service, and with the help of the becchini hastily dumped the body in the first open grave they could find. It was worse for the poor. They stayed in their homes, where they sickened by the thousand each day, and, being without help of any kind, could not hope to escape death. They died at all hours in the streets; those who died at home were not missed by their neighbours, until they noticed the stench of their putrefying bodies; the whole city was a sepulchre.

'It was common practice for people, moved more by fear of contamination than by charity towards the deceased, to drag the corpses out of the houses with their own hands, aided, perhaps, by a porter (if there was a porter was to be had), and to lay the bodies in front of the houses, where any funeral cart that made the rounds might have seen them. Sometimes, in the morning, there would be more dead piled up in the streets than the cart driver could count; often, whole families were loaded onto the biers. Priests arrived to find that they were burying not one, but six or eight, sometimes more. People had become indifferent to the suffering all round them, and the dead were disposed of as if they were goats.

'There was not enough consecrated ground for the vast number of corpses which day and night - almost every hour - were brought to the churches for burial. When the cemeteries were full, they dug a huge trench which they put the new corpses in as they arrived by the hundred, piling them up like goods in the hold of a ship, tier upon tier, each layer of bodies covered with a little earth, until the trench could hold no more.

'The surrounding countryside suffered as harshly as the city. There, in villages, or in open fields, by the roadside, on the farm, in the home, the unfortunate husbandmen and their families, bereft of doctors' or servants' care, died day and night, not as men, but rather as beasts. They too, like the Florentines, abandoned normality, believing each day to be their last, and stopped working in the fields and tending their animals, and instead drank and ate all they had stored. They denied shelter to their cattle, sheep, goats, pigs, fowl, even to their dogs, and drove them out into the fields to roam in the unreaped corn.

'But enough of the country! What we need to add (reverting to the city) is that so grievous was the judgment of heaven, that, together with the meanness of man, it is estimated that between March and July more than a hundred thousand people lost their lives within the walls of Florence. How many grand palaces, how many stately homes, how many splendid villas, once full of retainers, lords and ladies, were now left desolate and empty. How many old families, with vast tracts of ancestral land, with untold wealth, found that they now had no heir! How many brave men, how many fair ladies, both young and old, whom any physician - even if he were Galen, Hippocrates or Aesculapius himself - would have pronounced in the soundest of health in the morning, but were dead when evening came!'

Boccaccio, like other writers of the period, tends to overestimate number of casualties, but in essence, his descriptions of the ravages of the pandemic are accurate.

He states that 100,000 Florentines died; in reality, it was probably more in the region of half that number. Large numbers were used to signify that a lot of people had died, not that that was the exact count of casualties. Similarly, his pigs who dropped dead after chewing the clothes of a plague victim in the street may be poetic license in the same sense that a dog wielding a sword appeared in the streets of Messina in Michael of Piazza's chronicle. Fact and the tendency to use symbolic characters or creatures figures in many plague accounts. To the mediaeval mind, this would have been mere reportage; the terrors of Divine punishment were all too real to them, indeed, it seemed to be all around them in 1348, and accounts of devils, dogs with swords and other Fortean phenomena would have been read as meaning that things were about as bad as they could get. The Black Death taxed the limits of both language and imagination: it really was almost too terrifying to be described.

In fleeing to the countryside, those Florentines who could were setting a trend that would be repeated as the Black Death spread throughout Europe. Houses and possessions would be abandoned, the sick were left untended, animals wandered in the streets and the fields. There was almost no defence – or chance of escape - for the poor, who tended to live in the most crowded and unsanitary conditions. In addition, the disease would have found a further ally in the malnutrition that attended such quarters. To belong to the urban poor was, in effect, a virtual death sentence. If that wasn't enough, criminal elements such as the Becchini, perhaps some of whom were amongst those released in the amnesty from prisons, took advantage of the suffering and threatened the healthy with contamination unless a ransom was paid. Likewise, it was not unheard of for priests, gravediggers and undertakers to demand large and sudden pay rises before continuing their work.

Although mortality tended to be higher in major urban centres like Florence, the countryside was by no means immune. In Tuscany, as many people died in the villages as in the cities. A thinly spread population was no means of protection from the plague. And not only humans died: the Black Death

struck cats and dogs, sheep and horses. The fields were lit-
tered with decaying corpses amid the untended crops.

The Plague in other Italian cities

In Venice, six hundred people a day were said to be dying
at the height of the outbreak. Along with its rival Genoa, it
was one of the main ports of entry into Europe for goods
from the East. It also suffered repeated outbreaks of disease,
with a major outbreak of one sort or another occurring on
average every decade. The Council convened by the Doge,
Andrea Dandolo, on 20 March 1348 opted to open new burial
sites in locations that were both accessible but remote, at St
Erasmo in the Lido, and at St Marco Boccacalme. One chronicle notes that 'boats were hired at great expense to carry
bodies to the islands and the city was virtually deserted.'
Endless fleets of funeral barges took coffins to these new
cemeteries; they were soon filled. Immigration controls were
introduced, with a forty day quarantine period being required
of all those returning to Venice from the East (the figure forty
being chosen as it was the number of days Christ endured the
wilderness). As in Florence, minor felons such as debtors
were freed from jail, and surgeons were allowed to practice
medicine. However, the doctors were amongst the first to die;
those that survived did so because they adopted the precautionary measures of Boccaccio's characters. In other words,
they fled as far away as possible.

In convening the Great Council, the Doge was setting an
example that was to be followed by other Italian cities. All
recommended largely the same measures, such as the open-
ing of new burial pits, decreeing at the same time how deep
the bodies should be buried and how closely they should be
piled on top of each other; the banning of all social gatherings
such as weddings or gambling (processions and prayers were

seen as precautionary measures against the plague and were therefore usually allowed); the establishment of quarantine and travel restrictions; the prohibition of tolling bells or of town criers announcing anything at all; the removal of waste matter from the streets – corpses, rotten produce from market stalls. Sometimes, mob decisions were taken, such as in Milan. The first known victims there met a doubly unfortunate fate. Once it became known that theirs was a plague house, their doors were daubed with crosses – the traditional sign that a house was infected – and they were walled up inside it and left to rot. Frequently, however, these councils' efforts to try and stop the spread of the plague were like a child trying to empty the oceans with a bucket; more often than not, there were not even enough people left alive to see that these perfectly reasonable measures were carried out.

The town of Pistoia provides a good example of how the city fathers coped with the crisis, as here the civil ordinances published during the Black Death have survived. On May 2 1348, when the first reports of cases were coming in, the council drew up its first set of preventative measures. No one was to visit any area where plague was already raging, such as Pisa; if anyone was already there, they were forbidden to come back. No goods were to be imported into the town, including corpses. Markets were monitored closely, with only local produce being allowed to be offered for sale. Funerals were to be family-only affairs, and bells were not to be rung. Town criers and trumpeters were likewise silenced. Three weeks later, on May 23, the travel restrictions were lifted, as by now, regardless of whether one went to Pisa or not, one was just as likely to catch the plague in Pistoia. Food regulations, on the other hand, were tightened up. On June 4, a team of town gravediggers were appointed; no one else was to bury bodies but these 16 men. On 13 June, the rules for the defence of the town were re-drafted, to allow the rich to choose a proxy to serve in the ranks for them if they so desired. This discrimination is unusual, as despite their obvious advantages of wealth, Church and State did their inadequate best to protect all members of society - rich and poor alike - during the Black Death.

Although in Pistoia, the council did as much as they could to limit the damage, in Orvieto the council performed less conscientiously. The town had around 12,000 inhabitants and had been prosperous, despite heavy losses incurred during the ceaseless struggles between the Guelphs and the Ghibellines. The political uncertainty and instability this produced, in addition to the famines of 1346 and 1347, had crippled Orvieto's economy, and by the time the Black Death struck in the spring of 1348, the average Orvietan was in no mood for yet more disaster. The town council met on March 12, and all mention of disaster was studiously avoided. The plague was raging eighty miles away in Florence, and perhaps they felt that there was nothing they could do to avoid it. The town had one doctor and one surgeon, who both worked full time. There were also a good half dozen citizens who were qualified in medicine who could be prevailed upon to offer their services as and when the need arose. For a town of Orvieto's size, this was not bad going. There was only one properly equipped hospital, however, with several other institutions managing as best they could on private donations and worse facilities. Public hygiene, as in most mediaeval cities, was virtually non-existent. In repeated – and seemingly ineffectual - ordinances, the council forbade such traditional street activities as the rearing of animals, the tanning of skins, or the disposal of waste from windows.

The Black Death hit Orvieto particularly hard: around fifty per cent of the population were dead within three months of its arrival in April 1348. Unlike Pistoia, no ordinances were published with preventative measures. In fact, the plague does not appear in city records until June, when a new council was elected. But it was too late: the plague was raging at near to full strength, and of the seven councillors elected, two were dead by July 23. Three more were in their graves by August 7. Any pretence at trying to hold council meetings were scrapped; even the city's most important religious ceremony, the procession of the Assumption, had to be abandoned.

In Siena, work had to be halted on the new cathedral. The Black Death struck just as the transept had been built and the foundations of the choir and the nave had been laid; the masons died and no one was left to continue their work. The wool industry effectively ceased to exist, and the import of oil was halted. On June 2, all Siena's courthouses were closed down for three months, and gambling was banned for all time. (The loss of revenue was so great however, that this prohibition had to be repealed six months later when the worst of the epidemic was past.) So much money was bequeathed to the church in inheritances and donations (made no doubt with the salvation of at least the donor in mind), that all the regular taxes that the Church collected were suspended until 1350.

One of the most well-known of Siennese plague chronicles was written by Agnolo di Tura. 'Father abandoned child,' he writes, 'wife, husband; one brother, another, for this illness seemed to strike through the breath and the sight. And so they died. And no one could be found to bury the dead for money or for friendship... And in many places in Siena great pits were dug and piled deep with huge heaps of the dead... And I, Agnolo di Tura, called the Fat, buried my five children with my own hands, and so did many others likewise. And there were also so many dead throughout the city who were so sparsely covered with earth that the dogs dragged them out and devoured their bodies.'

Some merchants, fleeing across the Alps, tried to find safe haven in the Lombard town of Bobbio. They sold what goods they had, but either they themselves were carrying plague, or their merchandise was flea-infested, for the man who purchased their goods suddenly died, along with his entire family and several neighbours. One can only assume that the merchants must also have died, and been buried together in the common pit.

More woes from the same town are noted by de Mussis: 'one man, wanting to make his will, died along with the notary, the priest who heard his confession, and the people summoned to witness the will, and they were all buried together on the following day'.

In Piacenza, de Mussis' hometown, 'Cries and laments arise on all sides. Day after day one sees the Cross and the Host being carried about the city, and countless dead being buried... pits had to be dug in colonnades and piazzas, where nobody had ever been buried before.' Another chronicle notes 'the physician would not visit; the priest, panic-stricken, administered the sacraments with fear and trembling... no prayer, trumpet or bell summoned friends and neighbours to the funeral, nor was mass performed.'

In Padua 'the bodies even of noblemen lay unburied and many, at a price, were buried by poor wretches, without priests or candles.'

Chapter Three: Here Death is Chalking Doors with Crosses

The Black Death arrived in France only a month or two after it had begun its work in Italy. It is possible that the galley that brought the plague to Marseilles - the first town in France to be infected – was one of those that were driven from Genoa in January 1348, where they were last seen sailing westward. As their Italian neighbours had done, the Marseillese chased the galley from port with whatever means were at hand once it became evident that plague was rife amid the crew. The galley limped on, spreading plague along the coast, toward Spain.

France at the time was suffering from political troubles with its long-time adversary, England. A dispute between the two crowns over Edward III's continued possession of the Duchy of Guienne led to Edward claiming the throne of France for himself, which infuriated the French king, Philip VI. A truce had been agreed after the battle of Sluys, but this proved to be short-lived. Edward landed in Normandy and on 25 August the English won a decisive victory at Crécy, thus inaugurating the Hundred Years' War. In the long term, this bled the resources of both nations; it seemed to be a war, or series of conflicts, that seemed to have little purpose and that neither could win outright. In the short term, it severely damaged Philip's domestic policies and meant that, for the French peasant, subjected to looting and pillage by their own troops as well as the English, any sense of security and hope must have been destroyed.

In Marseilles, things rapidly got out of hand, with 56,000 casualties in the first month. Although this is a typically high contemporary estimate, it does seem that things were bad there, with both bubonic and pneumonic plague raging simultaneously. From there, two main lines of transmission branched out, west and north. The Western artery took the disease to Montpellier and Narbonne in February and March, and from there to Carcassonne, Toulouse and Montauban, reaching Bordeaux by August. The Northern route took the plague to Avignon in March; by summer it was at Lyons and it reached Paris by June.

Avignon, since becoming the seat of the Papacy in 1309, had become a thriving city, boasting some of Europe's finest architecture. In addition, Avignon was an important pilgrimage centre, and droves of the devout boosted the number of people present in the city, and made the crowded streets a prime area for transmission of the plague.

Contemporary reports speak of half of the population of the city being wiped out; another chronicle speaks of over 120,000 victims. These numbers, like almost all contemporary reports, should be taken with a pinch of salt; precise figures can only be gauged from whatever documents survive that strive for a certain level of objectivity. In the case of Avignon, the Rolls of the Apostolic Chamber record that 94 out of 450 members of the Papal Curia died during the Black Death. This level of mortality, 21%, cannot however be applied to Avignon's churchmen as a whole, as the well-fed Papal delegates should have had the means to cloister themselves from the plague in a way that the monk in the communal confines of a monastery or the itinerant friar would not. What can be gleaned from these figures, however, is that if one fifth of the city's richest, best housed and well-fed members died, it indicates that overall mortality in the rest of Avignon, amongst the poor, malnourished and ill-housed, would have been significantly greater.

Pope Clement VI himself had decided on the sequestering option, retiring to his chambers and admitting no one to his presence. He spent his time sitting in between two fires, and later decamped to his castle in the Rhône valley. Although running away does generally not have a good press, Clement, like most people, decided that staying alive was preferable to dying of a terrible and inexplicable disease. Moreover, he felt that he was more use to his flock alive, and that a leaderless church at such a dark time in the history of the world would not be a good thing. In a bid to make life less difficult for the suffering faithful, he made it easier for people to obtain absolution, and advised that litanies should be sung in procession several days a week. Clement took part in the earliest processions, but crowded streets, however, are dangerous places in times of plague, and they were soon abandoned in the name of public - and pontifical - safety.

Although Clement seems to have done all he could given the circumstances, the Church during the Black Death was in a tight corner. The duties of priests necessarily entailed dealing with the sick and they, along with the doctors, proved to be the two professions with the highest mortality rates. Despite this, priests in many areas were unpopular, as they were seen as agents of a Church that could not stop the plague. If the intercessions of the Church to the Almighty were having no affect, then that either meant the Church was not interceding hard enough on behalf of its people, or that God had abandoned the Church, disgusted like the peasant at its enormous wealth and opulence and its zealous pursuit of worldly power.

Mediaeval Medical Theories

The Church had also interfered in medicine, to say nothing of learning in general. When a person was ill, tradition dictated that the priest should be summoned before the doctor. If a doctor did find himself first on the scene, the first thing he had to establish was whether or not the ill person had confessed. If they hadn't, the priest would have to be called before the doctor could begin his work. Confession, unction and all the necessary prayers often took so long that the doctor would merely have to note that the patient had by now expired and he would have to go home again. During the Black Death, it was hardly surprising that doctors and priests perished in such numbers, as to die an improper death, without a blessing, was a death to be feared.

The average doctor, then, even if he could actually get in to see a patient once the priest had left, had few options open to him at the best of times and, in the case of a plague victim, almost none at all. What medical training there was in such great medical centres as Paris and Montpellier was dictated by the Church. In 1300, Pope Boniface had issued a Bull forbidding the mutilation of corpses. Although aimed at the excesses of relic hunters and tomb raiders, it effectively meant that surgery, post mortems and dissection classes were also anathema. The medical faculty at Paris, perhaps hoping to curry favour with the pope, declared itself opposed to surgery whereas at Montpellier, whether to placate would-be forward-thinking doctors or just out of rebelliousness, dissection classes were held. One every two years.

Mediaeval medical theory was almost entirely derived from the canonical figures of Hippocrates and Galen. Almost no attempt was made – in the West at least – to advance upon the work of these two giants of antiquity. (It may well have been their status as giants from antiquity that made people shy away from research, lest the masters should be proved wrong.) The world to them was comprised of elements and humours, and every condition that the human being could suffer from was due to an unfavourable combination of them. Ibn Khâtimah thought that people of hot, moist temperaments were most at risk during outbreaks of plague, especially sensuous young women of a passionate disposition, and the young and corpulent of either sex. Purging the system through emetics or the letting of blood was commonplace, as it was felt that any foul humours within the body could be thus released, benefiting the patient and aiding a swift recovery. It was not unheard of, either, for doctors to simply cut buboes off; the pain must have been unimaginable.

Philip VI commissioned the hallowed Medical Faculty at the University of Paris to find out exactly what had caused the unparalled calamity of the Black Death, and they quickly reported back to him with their findings. The cause, it seemed, was astrological in nature, not medical: an unfavourable conjunction of Saturn, Jupiter and Mars that took place in Aquarius at 1pm on March 20 1345 seemed to be at the root of all their suffering. Conjunctions of Jupiter and Saturn were bringers of death, and the added presence of the fiery Mars would indicate that, had they but known it three years earlier, disaster was bearing down upon them.

Despite their astrological prowess, the Faculty could say little on how to treat a plague victim. Their report is one of around twenty that survive from the period either during, or immediately after, the Black Death. The general feeling was that the epidemic had been caused by the corruption of the atmosphere, and the plague spread from place to place like a cloud of poison gas. One theory held that this miasma was caused by the sea becoming choked with dead fish. Another believed that the noxious atmosphere was caused by corpses that had lain too long unburied after a war that had no doubt been raging recently somewhere in the East.

There was agreement on the symptoms. Doctors dreaded the black welts in the armpits and groin, and they knew that if the patient spat blood – had pneumonic plague - then there was no chance of recovery. The Arab doctor Ibn Khâtimah, who witnessed the effects of the plague at first hand in Almeira, was almost alone in believing that the plague was infectious, and that pneumonic plague spread more rapidly than bubonic. Ibn Habib must have realised the infectiousness of victims coughing up blood and exhaling plague bacilli in the process when he described people spitting blood in Cairo as 'messengers drawing others to death.'

There was also general agreement that the best form of defence was isolation, to which added doses of frequent prayer would be advisable. Houses should be away from the coast, and preferably face north. Windows should be ideally covered with thick curtains or drapes to keep any infested air out of the house. (This would later cause a steep rise in the manufacture of tapestried heavy curtains that those who could afford them had installed to prevent any future outbreak.) To aid the atmosphere within the house, it was recommended that scented woods were to be burnt; juniper, ash, vine and rosemary were thought to be the most pleasant and therefore effective. Other authorities disagreed, believing that breathing in fetid air would grant immunity.

Whether or not one had achieved isolation, the best thing one could do was to do nothing. It was thought that sudden movements or unnecessary exertion would only leave one vulnerable, and many commentators argued that the less one did, the better. In addition, one should try and entertain pleasant thoughts, perhaps engage in conversation about the finer things in life, and keep one's mind from dwelling on what may be happening to one's neighbour.

The subject of diet produced a number of recommendations. Figs were thought to be good before breakfast, while Gentile of Foligno urged ingesting powdered emerald; on another occasion, he championed lettuce, which the Faculty of Medicine in Paris seemed to object to more strongly than his pronouncements about grinding up precious stones. Ibn Khâtimah thought that fresh fruit and vegetables were beneficial, but no one else agreed. He also advised getting a good night's sleep, reading the Koran every day and consuming cooked plums to avoid constipation. Another Arab treatise, by Yûhannâ ibn Mâsawayh, advised sucking acrid pomegranates and eating pickled onions for breakfast.

Paris and the rest of France

Despite the valiant attempts of doctors to understand and treat the plague, the Black Death continued to reap a vast harvest as it moved northwards into Paris, the city that boasted more qualified physicians than any other in Europe. Unfortunately, this was of no immediate benefit to the Parisians, as legacies bequeathed to the parish of St Germain l'Auxerrois clearly show. From Easter 1340 up to the middle of June, 1348, when the first cases appeared in the French capital, 78 bequests had been made to the church. During the next nine months, there were 419, an amount 40 times as high.

The *Chronicle* of William of Nangis, perhaps the best contemporary account of what happened in Paris, records that 'There was so great a mortality among people of both sexes... that it was hardly possible to bury them. In the Hôtel-Dieu de Paris...for a long time more than five hundred corpses were carted daily to the churchyard of St Innocent to be buried. And those holy sisters, having no fear of death, tended the sick with all sweetness and humility, putting all fear behind their back. The greater number of these sisters, many times renewed by death, now rest in peace with Christ.' Although five hundred deaths a day in one parish alone seems like a typically inflated mediaeval figure (it has been suggested that this is a misprint of 50), the death toll in Paris was severe, with perhaps as many as 50,000 people dying during the second half of 1348.

The rich fled, leaving the poor to face the brunt of the plague as it stalked the narrow streets. William of Nangis records that priests fled, too, making his 'holy sisters', who no doubt went to the grave in their droves while attempting to alleviate the suffering that raged around them, all the more remarkable. Some people reacted with less than Christian actions: they knew they were going to die, so they decided to spend what little time remained to them drinking and dancing. Looting and licentious living were commonplace, even more so than in Florence. To a casual observer, there can have seemed to be little difference between plague victims experiencing the feverish convulsions known as the dance of death, the *Danse Macabre* that inspired countless paintings, and those who staggered out into the street too drunk to walk in a straight line or even care. When even Pope Clement had agreed that the plague had been sent by God as a punishment for their collective sins, what use was it in trying to remain alive? Eat drink and be merry, for tomorrow we die.

The king had decided upon another course of action, and fled Paris with his retinue, seeking refuge in Normandy. It was no use: the plague followed them. The Duke donated land for a new graveyard after existing cemeteries were quickly filled. At La Graverie, there were not enough people left alive to bury the dead, and 'the bodies of the dead decayed in putrefaction on the pallets where they had breathed their last', as one chronicle reported. In La Graverie, as in all the other worst affected villages in Normandy, a black flag was flown from the church to warn travellers not to enter.

Despite not finding a haven on the north coast, King Philip did at least manage to stay alive. There was, however, a Royal victim in Bordeaux. In an attempt to strengthen ties between England and Castile, Edward III decided to marry off his 15-year-old daughter Princess Joan to the Castilian Prince Pedro. When they elected to stay at Bordeaux en route, the mayor, Raymond de Bisquale, installed them in the Chateau de l'Ombriere which overlooked the port. Unfortunately, the port was the epicentre of the plague in Bordeaux, and the death of Joan's chancellor, Robert Bourchier, on 20 August, must have made the Royal party acutely aware of the danger now faced by the princess. They decided to sit it out. But the chateau did not provide sufficient immunity and the princess died on 2 September. Her courtier Andrew Ullford left at once for London, where he reported the news to the King on 1 October. Edward ordered his daughter's body to be retrieved, and a party was duly despatched to Bordeaux. When they got there, they found that the situation had gotten so bad that de Bisquale, in an attempt to halt the spread of the infection, had had the entire port area burned to the ground. Unsurprisingly, the fire got out of control, and a number of other buildings were razed, including the Chateau de l'Ombriere. Princess Joan's body was never recovered.

Chapter Four: Satan Triumphant

The plague reached Germany in June 1348. Central Europe seems to have been hit from three directions at once, as the infection spread east from France, and northwards from Italy and the Balkans. Bavaria was affected first, with the disease continuing its march north and reaching Hamburg and the Hanseatic ports by the end of that year. The *Neuburg Chronicle* recorded that survivors of the pestilence were driven mad through despair, and took to wandering in the streets. Even animals were shocked at how bad thing had got, with wolves fleeing in fear from the towns and returning to the mountains.

In Frankfurt-am-Main, there were 2,000 deaths in 72 days; in Mainz, 6,000 people died; in Munster, 11,000; in Erfurt 12,000, while in Bremen, four parishes lost 7,000 souls between them. In Vienna, which was attacked in the spring of 1349, there were around 500 deaths a day, which peaked, according to the historian Sticker, with 960 people losing their lives in a single day.

In Vienna, the Black Death was personified as the Pest Jungfrau, a beautiful maiden who flew through the air in the form of a blue flame and killed people by simply raising her hand. When her victims expired, they were seen to exhale a blue flame, which was taken to be the Jungfrau's departure as she sought her next victim. In Lithuania, there was a similar legend: that the plague was a woman who killed her victims by waving a red scarf at their windows or doors. She was defeated by the sacrifice of a local man who waited for her all night in his home. When she arrived, he opened the window to her. She waved her scarf at him, and as she did so, he cut off her hand with his sword. He died, but the rest of the village was saved, and the scarf was preserved for many years in the local church as a relic of their miraculous escaped from the plague.

One seeming anomaly in Germany is the high numbers of priests who died during the epidemic. At least 35% of the higher clergy died during the Black Death. This would be the sort of figure one would normally associate with the humble parish priest called out day and night to administer the last sacraments and hear confession before they too succumbed to the disease, and not with their better-protected superiors, who were not coming into contact with the diseased and dying on a daily basis. The only possible explanation is that the German clergy performed their duties more conscientiously than their contemporaries elsewhere, and paid the price.

The church experienced further difficulties in losing monks and priests to worldly ways; the monastery at Ulm was said to have lost all its wealth through riotous living. Perhaps the monks realised, like so many people, that their days were numbered, so they may as well celebrate while they still had the time. The combined result of this depopulation was that, by 1350, the German church found itself decidedly short-staffed, with many priests having to serve more than one parish. In one district, for example, 39 benefices were held by 13 men in 1347, but after the Black Death, this had risen to 57 benefices held by 12 men. In need of manpower, the church was in no position to be choosy about new recruits, with the result that many new priests were young, ill-trained clerics. To make the situation worse, the many legacies and bequests that the church had received during the plague had greatly bolstered its financial position; it was now worse run and richer than before, leading it to be widely despised. Ultimately reform would come in the shape of Martin Luther.

The Flagellants

One of the most extraordinary by-products of the Black Death were the pilgrimages of the Brethren of the Cross, otherwise known as the Brotherhood of the Flagellants, which reached their peak in Germany during 1348 and 1349. They were travelling groups who performed acts of public self-flagellation as penance for the individual and collective sins that had brought the unimaginable suffering of the Black Death upon Europe.

Although the practice of flagellation is ancient, it is not noted in mediaeval times until 11th Century Italy, when it began to be practiced in certain monasteries. The immediate precursors of the Brethren seem to be the revolutionary flagellant groups of the mid-13th century. One such group, led by a hermit from Perugia called Raniero, felt that God's anger had been provoked by the manifold sins of the Italians, and claimed angelic support in a letter allegedly delivered by an angel in 1260. The letter claimed that God had been planning to destroy humanity altogether, but was convinced otherwise by the Virgin Mary, who pointed out the piousness of the flagellants led by Raniero.

The flagellants were on the move again in 1334, with another crusade before the decade was out. Perhaps inspired by the dire crop failures of a few years earlier and the worsening political climate in Italy, this particular pilgrimage was accused of heresy and their leader, a 'virtuous and beautiful maid', was sentenced to be burnt at the stake for her penitential activities. In the event, she was pardoned, but it would prove to be an ominous foreshadowing of events that would be repeated on a larger and - bloodier - scale in the 1340s.

The Brethren of the Cross are traditionally held to have emerged from Eastern Europe, the home of the earlier Bogomil heresy, founded by a group of 'gigantic women from Hungary'. They firmly believed that the Black Death had been sent by God as a punishment and, like Raniero's follow-ers, could claim angelic authorisation for their mission. An angel – whether it was the same one who sanctioned Rani-ero's pilgrimages or not is unclear – delivered a letter almost identical to Raniero's to St Peter's church in Jerusalem in 1343. The text differs slightly from the earlier version in that it specifically says that the Black Death had been sent as a Divine punishment, and that it was the Brethren's job to atone for humanity's sins.

The flagellants marched, usually in silence, two by two, usually in numbers of 200-300, although sometimes their numbers could swell to more than 1,000. The men marched first, the women at the rear. When they came to a town, they would head for the church, where the bells would be rung to announce their arrival. The church would be put at the Breth-ren's disposal, where they would recite their litanies, before moving into an open space - the town square or market – for the scourging. The ritual would begin with the members of the Brethren forming a circle and stripping to the waist. They would then march around the circle before the Master gave the signal to throw themselves to the ground, where they would usually adopt the posture of the Crucifixion. (It was not unknown for other positions to be taken - an adulterer might lie face down, or a perjurer would lie on their side and hold three fingers aloft.) The Master would move among them and thrash them. After this, the collective flagellation would begin. Each member of the Brethren had their own personal scourge, which would be made of three or four leather straps capped by a sharp metal stud. They would start to beat themselves around the upper body as three members of the Brethren, acting as cheerleaders, would sing hymns as the group thrashed themselves until they drew blood. The Master moved among the faithful urging them to pray for the souls of all sinners and after each bout of self-torture, they would throw themselves to the ground again. During all of this, the townspeople would stand watching, maybe even joining in with the hymns. Some felt that to be present at one of the Brethren's performances would ensure that divine mercy was bestowed upon them, and they were even thought to be able to work miracles. (One member even claimed to have been brought back from the dead during a ceremony.) People freely confessed their sins. After the members of the Brethren had thrown themselves to the ground, and after the required numbers of prayers, they would rise to their feet and begin the whole process again.

The pilgrimages were supposed to last 33 days (the figure being chosen as it is Christ's traditional age at the Crucifixion), with the scourgings taking places three times daily: twice during the day and once at night. In addition to the self-mutilation, the flagellants had to vow not to bathe for the duration of the pilgrimage, change their clothes, sleep in a bed or converse with the opposite sex. Participants also had to pay four pence a day for these privileges (in order to pay for food), confess all their sins since the age of seven, and also to provide evidence of their spouse's or family's approval before joining up. The charges excluded the poorer members of society from enlisting, while the strict rules kept out the insincere.

Despite their obvious sincerity, it is doubtful whether any member of the Brethren could have actually survived 33 days of self-administered torture, and it may have been the case that the really severe bouts of beating were only indulged in on special occasions. One witness, Henry of Herford, seemed to have attended one of the more extreme performances, as he records that some of the Brethren drove the metal studs of their scourges so far into their flesh that it would take a second tug to pull them out. Left unattended, the flagellant's wounds would quickly become septic. Even if medical attention had been encouraged, it is unlikely that any doctors would have had the time to attend the Brethren, since most were either trying to save victims of the plague or succumbing to it themselves.

During their first year of touring Europe, the Flagellants were widely welcomed, and even the Pope voiced his approval of their work. If they visited a plague-stricken town, then their visit would be seen as a possible way of appeasing God's anger. If the plague had not yet struck, then a visit by the Brethren might insure that the town remained plague-free. Initially, they were not expressly anti-clerical. The parish priest would be forced into being little more than a mere bystander in his own church as it was taken over by the Brethren; locals would no doubt enjoy seeing their priest taking so lowly a role. But as they visited more and more places – and their activities soon grew beyond the borders of Germany - their tone became increasingly messianic. They started to claim that the movement itself must last 33 years, after which would come the redemption of humanity and the arrival of the Millennium. They felt that they were an army of saints, whose job it was to save Christendom. It was claimed that they could drive out devils and heal the sick; some claimed to have had visions in which they conversed with Christ or the Virgin; rags and scraps of their bloodied clothing were treated like relics. The last straw was the claims by the Brethren's masters that they could absolve sins, and the movement started to entrench its anti-clerical position with the admission to its ranks of defrocked priests. The German flagellants began to denounce the Catholic church, and it was not unheard of for groups of them to interrupt services and drive the priest from the pulpit, which would inaugurate desecration and looting. This identified them as heretics, along with such groups as the Lollards, the Beghards and the Cellites, and they were increasingly seen as coming from the same popular tradition that was expecting the Holy Roman Emperor Frederick II to rise from the dead, destroy the Church and end poverty.

The desire to end poverty as well as plague meant that the Flagellants were also becoming increasingly anti-wealth. Any nobility and bourgeoisie who may once have sided with their cause now jumped ship as extremists increasingly dominated the movement. As the genuinely pious began to leave the movement, numbers were made up by the less spiritually inclined, with criminal elements joining up in order to travel incognito. If this was not enough, the plague began to appear amid the numbers of those on pilgrimage, and the Flagellants would take the infection with them from town to town.

Despite this, the numbers of people participating in Flagellant pilgrimages grew steadily until, by mid 1349, when they had already travelled through Hungary, Germany and Poland, one monastery in the Low Countries had to accommodate 2,500 Flagellants in the space of six months. 5,300 visited Tournai in half that time as plague ravaged the town. An enormous number, 42,000, were said to have gone to Constance. If anyone opposed them, or refused them entry into a town, they would be denounced as antichrists; near Meissen, one Dominican monk got into a dispute with the Brethren and was stoned to death. Certain areas managed to hold out. They were banned from the start by Archbishop Otto of Magdeburg from ever setting foot in his domain, and they never made much headway in either France or England. In France, King Philip had them turned back at Troyes, while in England, they never arrived in sufficient numbers to make much impact.

The turn of the tide came in the Papal Bull that Clement issued on 20 October 1349. Shortly after, a party of Flagellants arrived at Avignon, where they were threatened with excommunication. The rulers of Europe followed the Pope's lead and began to turn against the movement. The Bishop of Breslaw had a Flagellant Master burnt at the stake, while Manfred of Sicily let it be known that visiting Flagellants would be killed on sight. The movement seems to have gone very quiet after this, although a party of the Brethren visited Rome in 1350 during the Jubilee celebrations (which had been brought forward by fifty years to celebrate the disappearance of the plague), where their public penances seem to have gone unpunished, and the movement survived, albeit on a smaller scale, well into the 15th century.

The Persecution of the Jews

Despite their initial honourable aims, one of the more unsavoury aspects of the Flagellants' degeneration was the part they played in the persecution of the Jews. By this time, the movement was firmly in the grip of rabble-rousers and extremists who saw fit to exploit the popular theory that the plague was being spread by Jews who were poisoning Christian wells. That the accusers could then loot the Jews' property and steal their money was an added incentive. When the Flagellants arrived in Frankfurt in the summer of 1349, they went straight to the Jewish quarter and a massacre ensued. Even the news that they were approaching could be enough to spark off killings, as happened in Brussels, where 600 Jews were killed as the Flagellants drew near to the city's walls. Despite the part they played in the persecution, they did not, however, start it. That seems to have had its origins in France in the spring of the previous year.

Such was the fear and hatred of Jews, that, when the rumour that they were poisoning wells began to spread, Narbonne and Carcassonne promptly exterminated their Jewish communities. The theories became increasingly elaborate: that the Jews were in the pay of a mysterious cabal that had its headquarters in Toledo, that they poisoned the drinking water made from a powder imported from the Orient, and that this same cabal was also taking time to forge currency and kill Christian children. Other outsiders and social outcasts were also scapegoated. The English were viewed with some suspicion in France, while in Spain the Arabs found themselves accused. Lepers were also blamed, as they had been in the epidemic of 1321, when there had been mass burnings in Languedoc, but it was the Jew who was despised most of all.

A trial at Chillon later that year proved to be the decisive moment in determining the fate of Europe's Jews. In confessions extracted under torture, several Jews admitted poisoning wells, with the supposed poison being produced as evidence. Later that same month, on 21 September, Jews were banned forever from Zurich. In Basle, they herded them all into specially constructed wooden buildings and burned them to death. In the following months, there were massacres across Germany, with mass burnings beginning in November. At Speyer, the dead bodies were put into wine barrels and sent floating down the Rhine. Most killings took place when the plague was already raging, although at Strasbourg the following February, news that the plague was approaching was enough to launch an attack that left 2,000 dead. Clothes were torn from the victims' backs as the murderers searched in vain for the gold that was supposed to be hidden in the linings of the Jews' garments. In Mainz, the Jews took the initiative and killed two hundred Christians. The killings were avenged with the blood of 12,000 Jews. In some cases, the Jews destroyed their own property to deprive their persecutors of booty. At Esslingen in December 1348, they went one step further, and committed mass suicide by immolating themselves in the synagogue. As late as the spring of 1350, when the Black Death reached the Baltic, Jews were walled up and left to starve to death in the Hanseatic towns.

The Pope condemned the violence, threatening the persecutors with excommunication, but it had little effect. So deeply ingrained was the image of the Jew as the Satanic, baby-eating monster (largely propagated by Clement's predecessors at the time of the First Crusade) that his entreaties fell on deaf ears. Plague tractators and doctors, while not writing that the Jews were the cause of it all, nevertheless kept quiet, perhaps being unwilling to stand up for such a universally despised figure in European society. Ruprecht von der Pfalz took the Jews living on his lands under his personal protection and nearly provoked a revolution, earning himself the nickname 'Jew Master' in the process. Only Casimir, King of Poland seems to have been almost entirely successful in preventing slaughter in his lands. (He was said to have been under the thumb of Esther, his Jewish mistress.) The Jews would not experience such persecution again until the rise of Hitler, with many communities being wiped out, or permanently displaced.

Chapter Five: The Year of the Annihilation

The galleys that had infected Genoa and Marseilles had continued westward seeking landfall toward Spain. The Balearics were affected early on, with Majorca being infected in April 1348, around the same time that the pestilence was raging in the south of France. The effect of the plague was so bad that it left the Majorcans unable to defend themselves from pirate attacks and raids by the Bey of Tunis. They appealed to Pedro IV, the King of Aragon, for help, and Pedro agreed to provide troops on the condition they split the costs fifty-fifty. (To make matters worse, the crippled Majorcans were called upon the following year to provide troops to defend the even harder-hit Minorca.)

The plague seems to have reached the Iberian mainland a month after Majorca, with Barcelona and Valencia being among the first areas to be infected. The Spanish kingdoms were weakened by warring and conflict in much the same way as Italy, and were in no shape to cope with further disasters. Granada was racked by internal dissent and was suffering from general depression after defeats suffered at the hands of the Castilians. The Castilians, ironically, were stretched to breaking point through their additional siege of Gibraltar, which had exhausted King Alfonso XI's treasury and brought widespread poverty to the kingdom. The arrival of the Black Death made things drastically worse. So much money was bequeathed to the Church that the economy of Castile was threatened. King Pedro I decreed in 1351 that where relatives could be traced, the money must be returned.

In Aragon, Pedro IV's youngest daughter and niece succumbed to the plague in May, making them the first of Europe's royalty to die of plague. Further casualties followed in October, with Pedro's Queen also becoming a victim. King Alfonso of Castile was the only European monarch to die, catching the plague during the lengthy siege of Gibraltar and dying on 26 March 1350. The Arab armies of Gibraltar had been infected before their besieging Christian counterparts, and had thought of converting to Christianity as a preventative measure. It was only when plague began to move among the ranks of the Castilians did they realise that one's religion made no difference. God was punishing everyone.

The chronicler de Mussis records one of the best known plague stories. A pilgrim returning from Santiago de Compostella was passing through Salvatierra. In addition to the perils of pilgrimage – pilgrims were also suspected of having something to do with the alleged poisoned drinking water that had provoked the genocide against the Jews - armed robbers were at large, so he decided to stay the night at an inn and continue his journey at first light the next day. The establishment was run by a man and his two daughters, who, together with a single servant, were the sole survivors of their family. After dining with his hosts, who appeared to be in the best of health, he paid for his room in advance and went up to bed. The next morning he found that the man, his daughters and the servant had all died during the night. The pilgrim made it his business to leave in record time. To judge from this account, septicaemic plague, with its terrifying lack of visible symptoms (apart from sudden death, that is), seemed to be rife on the Iberian peninsula.

The great Arab physician Ibn Khâtimah witnessed the plague at first hand in Almeira. He was almost alone in believing that the plague was infectious, and noted that the arrival of plague victims in any given area would mean that the locals would also start to suffer within a few days. He also recorded that in Suq-al-Khalq, the mortality was almost 100%. This was a market area, where there was a lively trade in blankets, clothes and bedding, including that owned by plague victims. As business thrived, so did the plague. With each new transaction, the bacillus-carrying fleas that had made the cloth their home took the infection to fresh victims.

Although the Mediterranean coast was more badly affected than the Atlantic, Portugal did not survive unscathed. The city of Coimbra was decimated, and the great collegiate monastery of St Peter lost all its inhabitants within a week.

By the time the plague had reached Sicily in October 1347, it had already attacked the islands at the eastern end of the Mediterranean. The Byzantine historian Nicephoros Gregoras recorded that the plague attacked Rhodes and Cyprus, affecting not only humans but also animals, including horses, dogs and birds. This may support the theory that the Black Death was so devastating because it was either a mutation of normal plague, or that another disease that could attack the animal kingdom (not just rodents) was raging alongside it. Nicephoros's account is also one of the few to mention rats, noting that they too were dying in the houses they frequented.

On Cyprus, the largely Christian population thought the end of the world was upon them. Just as the first plague victims were noted, the island suffered a major earthquake, which caused a tidal wave that destroyed their fishing fleets and olive groves, upon which the island's economy depended. The upper echelons of Cypriot society were appalled to see three princes die within a week of each other. As the plague spread across the storm-damaged island, mortality became so great that bodies were not buried but simply thrown into the sea. Just in case their Arab slaves could somehow take advantage of the situation, they were all murdered before the Christian Cypriots tried to flee into the countryside, but, as happened on Sicily and elsewhere, the plague found them almost everywhere they went.

The Plague in North Africa and the Middle East

The trade routes that had brought the Black Death out of Asia to the Crimea and from there into Europe also seems to have been the main route of transmission into the Arab world. The Mongols of Sarai maintained a healthy economic relationship with Egypt, supplying them with two commodities that were almost certain to transmit the plague: slaves and the furs that were then fashionable in Mamluk society.

The Black Death reached Egypt in the autumn of 1347. It is possible that it came overland through Anatolia – where plague was rampant by 1348 – or along the sea route from the Crimea, via the Bosporus to Alexandria. This is perhaps more likely, as a ship put in at Alexandria around that time; out of the 300 slaves and crew and 32 merchants on board, there was only a single slave and 40 crew still alive. They all died in port. The disease spread throughout Alexandria, and had covered the whole of Lower Egypt by the spring of 1348.

The Arab world had experienced plagues before, from the legendary plagues suffered by the Egyptians, to the more historically verifiable Plague of Justinian, which had ripped through the Middle East during the sixth and seventh centuries. The first plague of the Muslim era was the Plague of Shîrawayh, which occurred in the fifth year of the Muslim calendar (627 and 628 by Christian reckoning), and was probably a recurrence of the Justinian plague. It broke out at Madâ'in, and among its notable victims were the Sassanian king Siroes, who died in 629. Plague seemed to recur with alarming frequency thereafter, claiming further kings and even some of the Companions of the Prophet, including Abû 'Ubaydah, Yazîd ibn Abî Sufyan, and Mu'ach ibn Jabal and his son. Outbreaks continued throughout the rule of the Umayyads (661-749), with caliphs usually retiring to their desert palaces when an epidemic occurred. It seems to have abated somewhat during the reign of their successors, the

Abbasids, and by the ninth century, with the works of Galen and Hippocrates now translated, Arab physicians were working to try and understand plague. The great doctor-alchemist Rhazes (866-925) was the first person to produce a description of pneumonic plague in Arabic by translating the work of Ahrun the Priest, who had witnessed the plague at first hand in Alexandria in 622. The time of Rhazes was a formative period in Islamic legal theory, which allowed the research that never happened to the same degree in the West until centuries later, when the stranglehold that the Catholic church had on scientific research was finally broken. Despite the admirable work done by Rhazes and his contemporaries, further outbreaks in 1056, 1063, 1157, 1200 and 1273 left them no better able to understand, or prevent, the disease.

The progress of the Black Death through Egypt and the Middle East left a depressingly familiar litany in its wake. Most of the main chroniclers resided in Alexandria, Cairo and Damascus, and it is from these cities that we have the most complete – and vivid – accounts of the ravages of the plague. In Buhayrah, no taxes were collected due to the number of dead. Animals died, and fields and crops were abandoned. The rural population shrank, both from plague deaths and migration to the cities, where a similar fate awaited all those who thought they could escape. In Damascus, the Governor ordered the destruction of all the city's dogs, as they were causing a further public health hazard in eating the dead bodies that lay unattended in the streets. Markets were deserted, and mosques were silent: there were no muezzins left to call the people to prayer.

Chronicles and poems written to commemorate and lament the catastrophe describe the suffering as vividly as Boccaccio did of Florence. Al Maq witnessed pneumonic plague in Cairo, where, he records, victims 'spat blood, uttered cries, and died'. As-Safadî is less terse: 'Then came the worst calamity that brought tears to the eye. People spat bits of blood, and one was covered with blotches and died... Every person in the morning or evening breathed out blood from his throat as if he had been slain without a knife'.

Death was everywhere, and there was endless trouble in burying the dead. There were constant shortages of coffins, causing the dead to be taken to the cemeteries and pits on planks (sometimes two or three bodies on a single plank), ladders, shutters from windows or even in large baskets. Failing that, camels – which were also susceptible to the plague - were used as hearses. The streets were constantly gridlocked with funeral processions; from every house came the wails of grief that are traditionally a part of Muslim funerals. At the mosque, things would be no better: they were packed to overflowing, and mass funerals were commonplace. Mosques were constantly busy with the observances of rites and crowds gathering for mass prayer recitals.

As in Europe, anything other than a proper burial was seen as a death to be avoided. It is true that when things got too bad, bodies were simply dumped in the Nile, although this was the exception rather than the rule. In contrast with certain cities of Europe – Paris for example, where society broke down completely for a period – Muslim society reacted to the disaster with stoicism and courage. Government stepped in to help wherever it could. In Egypt, the Sultan helped meet the costs of burial, and looking after the survivors. In Damascus, burial fees were abolished altogether. That is not to suggest that Muslim society did not have its rogues and profiteers: people left their jobs to become well-paid fulltime funeral givers and gravediggers.

The Muslim theories of the reasons for the plague were on the whole similar to those of their Christian counterparts. It was the will of God, who had seen fit to punish them, and they had no choice but to endure His punishment. A few commentators regarded it as a punishment only for the infidel; for the Muslim, it was a blessing and a martyrdom, in which the believer could easily demonstrate their faith by dying of plague. The other main difference of opinion was whether it was correct for a Muslim to flee an infected area, or stay and face the consequences. The Prophet had originally decreed during the Plague of Justinian that a Muslim must not flee a plague stricken land, nor enter one, which provided ample room for interpretation.

Mecca was infected in 1348, and proved another theological stumbling block, as the Prophet had also decreed that no disease would ever enter the holy cities of Mecca and Medina. Pilgrimage traffic had brought the great destruction to Mecca, and it was decided that there had to be unbelievers amid the pilgrim traffic. (That great numbers of true believers were also dropping like flies did not apparently dent this theory.) It was considered a miracle that it did not spread to Medina.

The Maghreb countries had been attacked from Sicily, which had infested Tunis in April 1348. Plague spread inexorably throughout Tunisia and Algeria to the Atlantic coast of Morocco. As usual, local politics were affected by the disease. The Marinid ruler of Fez, Abû I'Hassan, was trying to invade Tunisia at the time. His army was defeated by an alliance of nomadic tribes, but despite that, managed to move on to Tunis. According to the historian Ibn Khaldûn, 'a violent plague occurred and settled the affair'. At its height, the plague was said to be killing 1,000 people a day in Tunis. One of the similarities of Arab accounts with their Christian equivalents is the tendency to exaggerate the number of deaths. Nevertheless, Tunis in the summer of 1348 was not a good place to be. The Tunisian poet Abû I-Qasim ar-Rahawî laments the situation:

Constantly I ask God for forgiveness.

Gone is life and ease.

In Tunis, both in the morning and the evening –

And the morning belongs to God as does the evening –

There is fear and hunger and death,

Stirred up by tumult and pestilence.

The Arabs generally felt along with their European neighbours that the plague was spread through a miasma, floating slowly over the world to punish sinners. Isolation was sometimes seen as a solution, with certain nomadic tribes surviving by retreating far enough into the desert to avoid contact with outsiders. (The nomads who succumbed no doubt still had intercourse with others as they continued to work the trade routes.) In the Moroccan town of Salé, a certain Ibn Abu Madyan gave the idea of isolation an unusual twist: he walled himself up alive in his own home. He had enough food and drink laid in to last, he reasoned, and decided to sit out the plague. His gambit worked: he survived, no doubt emerging into a world very different from the one he had left.

Chapter Six: The Pestilence Tyme

More is known about the Black Death in England than in any other country. What is known tends to come from countries or cities where chroniclers lived, such as Boccaccio in Florence, and where there are no or few chroniclers – such as in Central Asia – information is scanty where it exists at all. But it is England, with its wealth of ecclesiastical and manorial rolls, that provides the most detailed picture of the pandemic. The Books of Institution record when priests were appointed to livings, and if that was due to the death, resignation or retirement of the previous incumbent, while the manorial rolls show when land changed hands from one person to another. From these facts an impression can be built up of how many people – clergy and laity alike – died in any area at any given time. The close connection between the two in the context of the Black Death is, of course, the need to confess one's sins and be absolved. Priests were at the frontline of the epidemic and paid for this very often with their lives.

Despite this, there is a great deal of confusion about when and where the Black Death entered England. That it arrived through the usual channel – a port – is beyond doubt, although precisely which port was accorded the dubious honour depends very much on the chronicler. Bristol and Southampton were believed by some to be the first parts of England to become infected, although scholars now believe that the town of Melcombe Regis (part of present day Weymouth) was the plague's entry point into the British Isles. At that time, Melcombe was an important port that provided as many ships for the siege of Calais as London or Bristol and, like most ports on the south coast, it was in almost daily contact with the continent and the Channel Islands, where the plague was already raging. *The Grey Friars' Chronicle* believed that the home port of the ship that brought the infection to Melcombe was Bristol, to which the ship took the disease after its departure from Dorset (reminiscent of Messina and Marseilles, although here it seems that the ship was not driven from harbour by burning arrows and siege engines).

The Chronicles also record various dates for the arrival of the Black Death. Dates given range from around the time of the feast of John the Baptist (24th June 1348) through to the autumn and even as late as Christmas. On 17th August, the Bishop of Bath and Wells ordered that processions be held every Friday and prayers said to protect his flock from the pestilence that was raging in 'the neighbouring kingdom'. Presumably he meant France, although, at a stretch, he may have meant the neighbouring diocese. Despite the confusion about the plague's origins, it was inevitable that it would reach Britain sooner or later. It must have arrived sometime over the summer, as it was raging with full force in Dorset by October. The Ecclesiastical records show that new vicars had to be appointed in Shaftesbury, for instance, due to the death of the previous incumbent, on 29 November, 10 December, 6 January [1349] and 12 May. In addition, in the six months after October 1348, 100 new vicars had to be appointed in the county as a whole.

At the time the Black Death hit Melcombe, England was a relatively stable and prosperous country. The Plantagenet king Edward III had won decisive victories against both the Scots and the French and, although he was never able to turn these triumphs to England's lasting advantage, it did provide a certain degree of stability and security. The wool and cloth industries were expanding so much that Edward had to start taxing exports in 1347. Around 85-90% of the population was rural, with the largest cities being London, with around 70-75,000 people, followed by Norwich (c.13, 000) and York (c.10,000). The village was the social unit most badly affected by the plague; some were wiped out altogether, all experienced lasting affects.

After the Black Death arrived in Dorset, it quickly spread throughout West Country. Bristol was attacked soon after, suggesting that the city was infected from the sea, rather than overland from Melcombe Regis. Its progress was haphazard, but by the end of the year, there was hardly a village in the South West that had not been affected. In January 1349, the Bishop of Bath and Wells was forced to take much more drastic action than his call for processions made the previous August, when he allowed people to confess to each other if no priest could be found (in other words, if the priest had himself died of the plague and had not yet been replaced). Confession could even be heard by a woman. The Bishop also notes in his letter that many priests were unwilling to take livings where the plague was known to be raging, or to visit the sick in their own parishes. Such an announcement from a senior churchman is ample indication that, by the beginning of 1349, the year the whole of England would be affected, the situation was already out of control.

Not long into the new year, the Black Death seemed to be everywhere in the south of England at once, with Wiltshire, Hampshire, Surrey, Sussex, Kent and East Anglia all being affected. In the West Country, Gloucester was the next major city to be hit after it had all but wiped out Bristol. Although Gloucester town council had placed an embargo on all traffic – human and otherwise - between themselves and the unfortunate Bristolians, it was, needless to say, a futile gesture. Between March and September, 80 parishes in the county lost their priests to the plague.

While Gloucester suffered, the Black Death took hold of central southern England. In Oxford, around 35% of the clergy died. Nicholas, the Abbot of Eynsham Abbey, fell victim, not to plague, but to dismissal; he was sacked by Bishop

Gynewell for an offence that has not been recorded. Two administrators were appointed to look after the abbey while a successor was chosen. On 13 May the Bishop was told that the first of the two men was dead, the second dying. To remedy the situation, the Bishop sent two more monks to Eynsham Abbey to replace them. Both died en route for the abbey and Gynewell decided to cut his losses and reinstate Nicholas.

Although the abbey suffered no less badly than elsewhere, two villages on its land fared worse. Coming to Tilgarsley ten years later, tax collectors reported that they could not collect any tax, as no one had lived there since 1350. What had once been a prosperous village was now a weed-choked ruin. In Woodeaton, all bar two of the villagers died. Rather than let it go to seed, Nicholas got new tenants in. Although they were paying a slightly higher rent, the new tenants were required to perform fewer feudal services.

At Cuxham near Thame, the force of the plague is grimly illustrated by the fate of the village reeves. Between 1288 and 1349, the village had had only two, albeit very long standing, reeves. The old reeve died in March that year, and his replacement lasted only a month before falling victim to the pestilence. The replacement's replacement managed to last twice as long as his predecessor, surviving until June. The third new reeve lasted a matter of weeks before dying in July; his replacement managed to survive a whole year, but by the following July was also dead.

The story was much the same everywhere. At Wycombe, around 60% of the clergy died. This is extremely high, and suggests that the overall death rate amongst the population was in the region of 50%. Durrington, near Amesbury, had lost 18 out of 41 of its tenants by the end of 1349. The Diocese of Winchester lost 48% of its clergy (the highest for a diocese in the whole country), and the Bishop ordered extra penances, with barefoot processions on Sunday, Wednesday and Friday. Deaths were running at such a level that the inhabitants of Winchester, fearing infection from the corpses piling up by the day, demanded that a new burial pit be opened outside the city walls. It was only when they attacked a monk who was conducting a funeral service in the grounds of the cathedral that the Bishop acceded to their demands (but not before excommunicating the mob).

'A voice in Rama has been heard', wrote the Bishop, 'much weeping and crying has sounded throughout the various countries of the globe. Nations, deprived of their children in the abyss of an unheard-of plague, refuse to be consoled because, as is terrible to hear, cities, towns, castles and villages... have been stripped of their population by the calamity of the said pestilence, more cruel than any two-edged sword. And into these said places now none dare enter but fly far from them as from the dens of wild beasts.' Nonetheless, the Bishop did rather well financially from the unheard-of plague. Death duties, which normally amounted to between £10-£20, now shot up fivefold, with 1349 producing a revenue of £101 14s 4d.

The Black Death in London

After Winchester, the ancient capital of England, had fallen to the plague, it was grimly inevitable that its successor, London, would be overrun. Although the story of the Black Death in England is largely the story of catastrophe in rural communities, the cities fared just as badly. Although not as big as Paris, Vienna, Bruges or Constantinople, with around 60,000 people living inside the city walls and another 10,000-15,000 living just outside, London was far and away England's biggest city, with the 13,000 strong Norwich running a distant second.

Three factors contributed greatly to the spread of the Black Death in London: poor (in many cases virtually non-existent) sanitation, dirt and overcrowding. These things in themselves did not directly cause the infection to spread, but resultant illnesses such as dysentery meant that the plague could do its work in bodies already weakened and wasted. Public hygiene was no better than in the village, in fact it was probably worse. It was common practice to dispose of waste matter of every kind in the street. In some cases, there would be a gutter in the middle of the street that would, in theory, carry the excrescence away; blockages were frequent. If the gutter or ditch did its job, the matter would be washed into either the Thames, or into a communal cesspit. The pits posed problems for the water supply, as they frequently leaked into wells that people drew their drinking water from. Many privies emptied either directly into the river, or, more commonly, a ditch. The Fleet Prison Ditch had eleven toilets and three sewers emptying into it. The accumulation of ordure became so bad that it prevented water from the Fleet flowing into the prison moat.

The Thames suffered as much refuse as the average street. Not only was there the continual influx of sewage, but also the waste matter from butcheries. The butchers of St Nicholas Shambles had been based near Fleet Prison, but the smell from the animal carcasses became so bad from 'putrid blood running down the streets and... bowels cast into the Thames' that they were obliged, by Royal decree, to move outside the city walls entirely.

London also suffered from a problem not encountered in the rural community that greatly aided the progress of the plague: that of overcrowding. Mediaeval London's 75,000 people lived in a space of little more than two square miles. In filthy bustling streets barely wide enough to allow two carts to pass, the Black Death found easy pickings. The poor would often live in the same room as their animals; the safety of isolation found by Boccaccio's characters was an impossibility for the urban poor.

The plague probably arrived in London in late 1348. It is not known whether it was brought by people escaping the situation in the shires, or arrived on incoming merchant ships. It may well have had several points of entry into the city. By the beginning of 1349, the existing graveyards were full and new ones were swiftly opened at Smithfield and Charterhouse. That plague was rife in the cold months of January and February suggests that the first wave of victims in London had developed pneumonic plague, with its bubonic variant not appearing until the warmer summer months that it tended to thrive in. Bodies in these mass pits would have been buried five or six deep, with a thin layer of soil separating each corpse from the one above it. There would have been dozens of bodies brought to the new cemeteries each day: the figure of two hundred daily recorded by Robert of Avesbury seems a little high, although not as high as that quoted by John Stow, who wrote that fifty thousand bodies were interred at Charterhouse alone, which would have been consistent with a total death toll of more than a hundred thousand. Given that the total population of the city and its immediate environs was around 75,000, Stow's figure would necessitate that a third of the population die twice. Needless to say, contemporary estimates, like those at Florence and elsewhere, tended to range between high and impossible. An exact figure of fatalities is not possible to establish, although it is not beyond the realms of probability that around 30,000 people died in London.

Although the poor were the plague's most frequent victims, the rich and powerful were not immune. John Stratford, the Archbishop of Canterbury, died in August 1348 as did his successor, John Offord, who died in May 1349 even before he could be enthroned. His successor, the prominent scholar

Thomas Bradwardine, returning from Avignon, also fell to the plague, dying on 26 August almost as soon as he had landed at Dover. There was a further ecclesiastical victim in the form of Simon de Bircheston, the Abbot of Westminster, who retreated in vain to his country house at Hampstead. Twenty-seven of his monks also died. The Royal family had already lost Princess Joan to the plague in Bordeaux the previous September; now it was the turn of Royal surgeon Roger de Heyton, who died on 13 May. Amongst the City livery companies, all eight wardens of the Company of Cutters were dead by the end of 1349; all six of the Hatters' Company's wardens were dead by May 1350, while the Goldsmiths' Company lost four of its wardens by the end of 1349.

The Plague in East Anglia and the North

After London, the plague spread mercilessly into East Anglia before turning northwards. In Norwich, the second largest city in the whole country, the death toll was above the national average, with over half the population perishing during the summer and autumn. In the whole diocese, there were around 80 new priests instituted each year. Between March 1349 and March 1350, the total rose to a staggering 831. In the neighbouring diocese of Ely, it was proportionally even worse, with 18 times as many institutions than in a normal year. Although the Church was massively overstaffed and replacement priests were usually no more than a few weeks in the coming, such appalling losses inevitably meant that standards would sooner or later slip, the new priests often being young, inexperienced, illiterate or morally suspect.

Although Norwich rapidly became an inferno of disease, the plague showed its erratic side as it moved north. Cambridge lost half its population, and within a ten-mile radius of the city, the villages of Oakington, Dry Drayton and Cottenham lost between 50% and 70% of their populations, but the neighbouring manors of Great Shelford and Elsworth hardly had any casualties at all. The county of Lincoln was decimated, with 15 villages being completely wiped out, yet Northamptonshire escaped lightly. Huntingdon was so badly affected that it was unable to pay its taxes, while Nottinghamshire experienced a lower than average mortality.

Although local authorities were taxed almost to breaking point, it seems that the machinery of government survived the onslaught. One bizarre indication of this comes from York. On 7 August 1349, an inquest recorded that one William Needler had died of the plague, and that there was nothing suspicious in the manner of his passing. What is remarkable is that it was felt necessary to hold an inquest into a death when the plague must have been raging at something close to its peak in the city. That it was possible to assemble a jury suggests that, however bad things got, people generally tried to carry on as best they could; perhaps this was the only way of coping with the cataclysm.

Records are scarce in the North of England. Repeated incursions by the Scots had left Northumberland and Cumbria demoralised even before the plague struck, the continual pillaging destroying clerical records amongst other things. Some facts survive: the lands of Carlisle Castle remained untended for eighteen months due to lack of labourers, while the city itself was relieved of its tax burden because it was 'depressed more than usual' due to the pestilence. In the county of Durham, Billingham lost over half its population, while West Thickley was wiped out; the Ecclesiastical rolls simply say 'they are all dead.' A peasant was said to have been driven mad through grief after losing his family to the plague, and spent many years afterwards wandering all over the county trying to find them. In Durham itself, there seems to have been a stand-off between tenants and landlords.

Although the situation had initially been beleaguered by the unwelcome attention of the Scots, the arrival of the plague was the breaking point, leading to the only incidence in the whole of England of the Black Death causing civil disorder.

The Plague in Scotland, Wales and Ireland

According to the chronicler Henry Knighton, when the news reached Scotland that a plague was killing vast numbers of the English, the Scots rejoiced, and decided that this would be a good moment to invade. As Scottish forces were about to launch their campaign from the forest of Selkirk, the plague suddenly appeared in their ranks. The soldiers panicked, and fled back to their homes, taking the infection with them. Although the progress of the disease seems to have been impeded by the winter of 1349/50, by the spring it was back at work. One of the few contemporary Scottish chronicles was that of John of Fordun: 'In the year 1350 there was, in the kingdom of Scotland, so great a pestilence and plague among men... as, from the beginning of the world even unto modern times, had never been heard of by man... nearly a third of mankind were thereby made to pay the debt of nature. Moreover, by God's will, this evil led to a strange and unwonted kind of death, insomuch that the flesh of the sick was somehow puffed out and swollen, and they dragged their earthly life out for barely two days.'

Fordun is interesting in that he believes that a third of the population perished. For a mediaeval account, this is surprisingly conservative, as most chroniclers were notoriously prone to exaggerate the number of fatalities. Most researchers believe that around a third of Britain's population perished between 1348 and 1350, which would mean either that Fordun is almost unique in his accuracy, or that he, too, is exaggerating. If that were the case, then it would mean that

Scotland suffered less severely than England, Wales or Ireland.

Wales seems to have been infected shortly after Bristol and Gloucestershire. It is quite possible that the disease spread simply by crossing the Severn into Monmouth. By March 1349, it was certainly in Abergavenny, where officials gave up any hope of collecting rent from tenants on the lord's land, as there were virtually none left alive. In Cardigan, out of 104 rent paying tenants, 97 were either dead or had fled (no doubt to die elsewhere) by June. As in England, the plague helped the manorial system to its grave.

From South Wales, the plague seems to have re-entered England, and then travelled north, re-entering the principality from Cheshire. Wales, then as now, was split between the English-speaking south, and the Welsh-speaking north, where the foreign invaders had never made any serious inroads. What records there are tend to come from the south; in the north they are almost entirely lacking. What little is known of the situation in the north suggests that things were very bad. The miners of Holywell, near Flint, were decimated; the few who survived downed tools and refused to go on working.

The Welsh poet Jeuan Gethin witnessed the plague at first hand in the spring of 1349. He compares the plague to black smoke, 'a rootless phantom which has no mercy', the buboes being 'a grievous ornament that breaks out in a rash', an 'ugly eruption that comes with unseemly haste', and, in what is possibly the only contemporary use of the term, 'early ornaments of black death'.

Things were similarly bad in Ireland. The infection was probably brought from Bristol, which was the main source of trade from England, although it could have come on a boat from France. Even less is known about exactly when the plague struck. The Archbishop of Armagh, Richard Fitzralph, visited Pope Clement at Avignon in August 1349, and reported that, although the plague had done disastrous damage to the English, the Scots and the Irish had so far escaped largely untouched. Probably unbeknownst to Fitzralph, things were getting bad back home even as he spoke. The Archbishop of Dublin died on 14 July, and the Bishop of Meath also went to meet his maker before the month's end.

Ireland, like Wales, had suffered from the incursions of the English, and was also recovering from a bloody civil war that had raged during the 1320s and 1330s. Here, as with the conflicts that had weakened Spain and Italy, one cannot help but feel for the ordinary people caught up, first by conflict, and then almost destroyed by apparent Divine Retribution. Survival, difficult enough at the best of times, now seemed a luxury that none could afford.

One of the few records from Ireland that survives is the *Kilkenny Chronicle*, written by a monk there, John Clyn. 'Plague stripped villages, towns and castles and swallowed them up. This pestilence was so contagious that those who touched the dead or the sick were immediately infected themselves and died, so that penitent and confessor were carried together to the grave…. Many died of boils, abscesses and pustules which erupted on the legs and in the armpits. Other died in frenzy, brought on by an affliction of the head, or vomiting blood.'

Clyn had no doubt seen his fellow monks perish (and buried them in all probability), and was writing in what must have seemed to be the end of the world. His account is made all the more poignant by the words, in another hand, that conclude it:

'And I, Brother John Clyn, of the Order of Friars Minor and of the convent of Kilkenny, wrote in this book those notable things which happened in my time which I saw with mine own eyes, or which I learned from people worthy of belief. And in case things which should be remembered perish with time and vanish from the memory of those who are to come after us, I, seeing so many evils and the whole world, as it were, placed within the grasp of Satan, being myself among the dead, waiting for death to visit me, have put into writing truthfully all the things that I have heard. And, lest the writing should perish with the writer and the work fail with the labourer, I leave parchments to continue this work, if perchance any man survive and any of the race of Adam escape this pestilence and carry on the work which I have begun.'

Below that, perhaps too ill to continue, he has simply written 'great dearth'. Another scribe has added, 'Here it seems that the author died.'

Chapter Seven: The Triumph of Death

In May 1349, a wool ship set sail from London, bound for the thriving Norwegian port of Bergen. While at sea, plague began to spread amongst the crew. By the time the ship ran aground near their destination, no one was left alive. A group of Norwegians boarded the vessel, perhaps curious as to what the hold may contain, possibly hoping for plunder, but instead took the infection ashore with them and, by September, the whole town of Bergen was in the throes of an outbreak.

The final months of the Black Death, between late 1349 and early 1351, saw it spread throughout the whole of Scandinavia (with the possible exception of Finland, which was well off the main trade routes). King Magnus II of Sweden ordered his people to fast on Fridays, and to process barefoot around cemeteries carrying relics. In Uppsala and Stockholm, mortalities were highest during the winter, suggesting that pneumonic plague was at work, which was able to thrive in colder temperatures. If this were the case, then it would seem likely that pneumonic plague also found further victims in Russia, which it reached just as the pandemic was finally ebbing in the rest of Europe. The Shetlands, Hebrides, Orkneys and Faroes were all similarly affected. Iceland had a lucky escape: a boat was bound for Reykjavik from Bergen, but mortality amongst the crew was so high that sailing was impossible. The Danish fishing outposts in Greenland seem to have experienced a population drop, although this may have been due to the inhabitants deciding to return home rather than remain in the Arctic, where the regular supply ships had all but ceased due to the effects of the plague.

The plague had often shown an erratic progress, attacking one town with exceptional virulence, but leaving its neighbour virtually untouched. Although descriptions of Northern

Italy bring to mind the images of Bosch and Breughel, Milan escaped more or less untouched. Whether this was due to the Milanese quarantine (the strictest in the whole of Italy) or potluck will never be known for certain. Other, much larger areas remained hardly affected, in particular Poland and Bohemia. Although these countries were not heavily involved in trade, and therefore escaped the inevitable death that the trade routes brought, subsequent outbreaks would not be so kind. Bohemia was ravaged in the first recurrence of the Black Death in 1361. Iceland, which came so close to infection in 1349, was almost wiped out in an outbreak in 1402. Why epidemics behave they way they do is still a mystery; with the passing of so much time, it will probably never be known why the Black Death behaved in the way it did.

The Effects of the Black Death

Between 1347 and 1351, it is estimated that the Black Death killed one third of the population of Europe. The death toll in Asia and the Middle East was of a similar magnitude. Put another way, between the earliest deaths in Mongolia in 1328 and the last fatalities in Moscow in 1351, fifty million people, one third of the known world, perished.

Remarkably, historians of the 19th century, and some well into the 20th, did not regard the disappearance of every third person as anything particularly significant. The opposite view was taken by G.M. Trevelyan, who believed that the Black Death was at least as important as the Industrial Revolution, and David Herlihy, who believed that without the Black Death, there would have been no Renaissance (and without a Renaissance, no Industrial Revolution). The prevailing view now is that the pandemic accelerated changes that would have happened anyway, and that it had profound and lasting consequences on the countries it ravaged; just what these consequences are, historians are still debating.

In the case of the best documented country, England, it can be seen from manorial and ecclesiastical records that somewhere between 30%-40% of the population died, with the average mortality amongst priests being slightly higher, around 45%. No precise population figures are known - there wasn't a census after the Domesday Book in 1087 until the Poll Tax of 1377 - but it is generally agreed that England, and indeed the whole of Europe, was overpopulated by the time the Black Death struck. The pandemic thinned out the population to more sustainable levels, and led to an increasingly ageing population. The same thing can be said of the continent as a whole, although possibly in Tuscany the death toll was something over the average.

Most towns in England seemed to recover with remarkable speed. One of the immediate effects of the plague was that wages rose by around 25%. There were not enough workers to till the land, and those that survived were able to demand a higher wage. It also meant that labour became more mobile: if a lord was not offering a good enough deal, the labourer could move onto the next town, village or parish. Sometimes agreements were made where an hereditary tenant – a serf – would be granted their freedom (in other words they were no longer tied to work for one lord but could move to a different manor or area entirely if they so chose), in exchange for lower rents, thereby tempting them to stay. This meant that the lord of the manor had the land worked, but that his workforce now had the option of leaving; the number of these freed serfs, called yeomen, increased greatly over time, ultimately leading to the end of the manorial system. (Yeomen would be the ancestors of what would today be called the middle classes.)

The post-plague years saw a gradual increase in standards of living for the yeomanry. Metal pots began to be used rather than earthenware ones; with more food available for fewer people, diet improved; women were able to do jobs that were previously denied to them, such as working in the brewing industry, as there were no longer enough men to do the work.

In education, there was a marked shift away from using Latin in the universities, towards teaching in the vernacular. Quite simply, there weren't enough people left who were fluent in Latin or French (the language spoken at Court): prior to 1348, education had been dependent upon older men who, when the plague struck, were largely wiped out. (Four of Europe's thirty universities vanished.) In their place came younger men and new institutions; in Cambridge, three new colleges were founded as result of the Black Death.

The Church was widely perceived as having let its flock down, not just in England, but across Europe. Multitudes of priests had died, bishops also, and therefore couldn't be special. They were just the same as their parishioners, full of the same vices, and just as mortal. That many priests had died doing their duty – no doubt full of mortal terror – never seemed to be an issue. What was commented upon, however, was that their replacements were worse educated, less devoted to their job and more interested in money and status.

The widespread growth in unorthodox forms of religion in the post-Black Death years can be directly attributed to this disenchantment with the Roman Church. Dissenters, Lollards and Wycliffites all emerged to fill the void left by the partial collapse of trust in the church. Wandering – called Mendicant – preachers proliferated, and were widely welcomed wherever they went. Not tied to worldly wealth or power, they were seen to be 'of the people' in a way that the average Catholic priest rarely could hope to be.

Shortly after the Black Death had subsided, a petition signed by various bishops calling for the outlawing of the mendicants was handed to Clement at Avignon. Remarkably, the Pope lashed out at his own clergy: 'If their preaching be stopped, about what can you preach to the people? If on humility, you yourselves are the proudest of the world, arrogant and given to pomp. If on poverty, you are the most grasping and the most covetous... If on chastity – but we will be silent on this, for God knows what each man does and how many of you satisfy your lusts.'

In the years after the Black Death, people began to make efforts to ensure that, however long they had left, they would be going to the right place when their time came. There was a huge surge in the number of new chapels built. Funeral clubs were established to make sure that even the poorest members of the parish received a proper burial. Masses were introduced against the plague, and the image of the weeping Mother of God, the Mater Dolorosa, who seemed to be weeping not just for Her Crucified Son, but for the sufferings of all humanity, became a popular figure to appeal to during times of plague, or if it was even threatened. A more personal type of Christianity began to emerge, as if each person was preoccupied with their own mortality. It is as if the gloomy-sounding advice dispensed by ascetics, 'think constantly of your own death', suddenly came to be widely heeded. Some of the best loved classics of English mysticism, such as the *Cloud of Unknowing* and the *Ladder of Perfection*, date from the years immediately after the Black Death. They are all from the pens of anchorites and mystics, and were frequently written to one specific individual advising them how best to ready their soul for the next world.

In art, Christ began to be portrayed more frequently either giving Judgement rather than Benediction, or on the Cross. Death and suffering became the subjects that every artist had to deal with. Images of St Sebastian and Job proliferated and the Danse Macabre – Death leading the living into his kingdom – was painted, sculpted and chiselled across Europe. In architecture, styles became simpler, more austere. The era of intricate Gothic churches was over. The best masons were all dead, and their successors either could not, or would not, copy their masters. An autumnal darkness had fallen across European art, which would not recede until the Renaissance.

The general sense of unease was exacerbated by the frequent return of the plague. There was another serious outbreak in 1361, which was also known as the Grey Death or the Children's Plague, as it was said to have killed huge numbers of children. Because it struck an already weakened society, it was nearly as catastrophic in its impact as the first visitation. 1369, 1371 and 1375 saw the plague return, and tensions in certain parts of society rose. Whether or not the Black Death caused the Peasant's Revolt of 1381 has long been open to question. There were similar uprisings in France and the Low Countries around the same time; perhaps, without the Black Death, these would have arisen later rather than sooner.

The immediate impact of the Black Death upon Muslim society seems to have been to cause severe economic disruption. In Egypt, anything directly related to the plague, such as shrouds, coffins, pharmaceuticals and labour went up in price. Luxury goods also suddenly became prohibitively expensive. Although the plague in Europe affected the structure of land ownership by accelerating the demise of the manorial system, no such change seems to have occurred in the Middle East. Furthermore, there seemed to be no large-scale collapse in public morality, as happened across Europe, and the Jews remained unmolested. For most Muslims, the Black Death was not an apocalyptic Divine punishment for humanity's sins, but was part of God's plan, and the best the believer could do was to keep the faith, and hope that the dark times would pass. They did not. Subsequent outbreaks of plague in the Middle East were to prove much more damaging in the long term than the Black Death.

Likewise in Europe, plague would be a feature of society for the next three hundred years. Subsequent outbreaks were usually localised, although they still managed to rage with some of the old ferocity. There were catastrophic outbreaks in London in 1563 and 1665. John Evelyn notes in his Diary for 7th September 1665: '[returned to London where] there are perishing near 10,000 poor creatures weekly… dangerous to see so many coffins exposed in the streets, now thin of people; the shops shut up, and all in mournful silence, not knowing whose turn it might be next.' This epidemic, known as The Great Plague to distinguish it from the horrors of the 1340s, did have a positive outcome of sorts: the following year the city suffered the Great Fire, and led to London being largely rebuilt. In the process, the sewage system, one of the Black Death's chief allies, was overhauled making London the most hygienic city in the World. The nursery rhyme 'Ring a ring a roses' is said to have originated with the Great Plague, although the earliest printed versions date from the nineteenth century. The 'ring a roses' were the livid blotches that appeared on the victim's skin after the buboes had appeared; the 'pocket full of posies' possibly flowers or herbs that the victim carried to ward off the stench of the dead (which, by purifying the air immediately around them, was also supposed to ward off the plague-carrying miasma); the 'atishoo atishoo/we all fall down' hardly needs elaborating.

Smallpox largely replaced plague as the chief killer from the 18th century onwards. Why this happened, no one is sure. But that was not to be the end of the plague.

The Third Pandemic

The third pandemic of plague began in China in the 1850s and incubated over a number of years until it reached the seaports in the early 1890s. From there, it was spread more rapidly around the globe, striking with particular virulence in India, Australasia, Egypt and North Africa, and South America. Hawaii suffered a severe outbreak in 1899, and San Francisco was affected in 1900-1904, and again in 1907-1909. The second outbreak there was exacerbated by unsanitary conditions following the earthquake of 1906. The third pandemic did not make much impact on the UK, although there were isolated cases in various ports such as Glasgow and Liverpool. Suffolk was affected in 1910, with two further deaths occurring in June 1918. Sporadic outbreaks continued worldwide for years, and officially the third pandemic was not considered over until 1959. However, outbreaks have continued, mainly in South America, Africa and Asia, and some researchers believe that these epidemics are still part of the third pandemic, which has yet to completely run its course.

Latest Research

The third pandemic offered scientists the chance to study plague properly for the first time, and research continues. Vaccines are now available to treat it, although these must be administered in the early stages if they are to work. It remains endemic in many parts of the world; in addition, the possible threat of its use in germ warfare ensures that those studying it remain fully funded and equipped.

That plague played a major part in the Black Death is generally still accepted, although it is now thought that something else was working in tandem with it. Either this was a new strain of plague, or was a virus similar to Ebola. One problem has been the speed with which rat and flea borne plague can travel: the Black Death was notorious for the speed at which it spread. Some researchers believe that this can be explained by the presence of a cattle disease such as anthrax. Rats and fleas would not be able to spread the infection on their own to remote rural areas such as Norway, but infected cattle could, as they were already there. Eating tainted meat would have finished the job. That there may have been some form of mediaeval CJD present in the plague has been confirmed by the recent discovery of anthrax spores in a plague pit in Edinburgh.

It is also possible that the Black Death was largely comprised of a virulent mutation of plague; perhaps it continues to mutate. New diseases, after all, are still occurring: AIDS has been the most high profile, and the most devastating. But there are puzzles: in July 1999 in Russia, in a village halfway between Volgograd and Rostov-on-Don, there was an outbreak of an unknown disease, something wholly new to medical science. Luckily the outbreak was contained and it has not (so far) recurred.

In September 1999, a conference was held to try and establish a strategy for the possible reappearance of plague in Britain. How would the beleaguered National Health Service cope? Would private health care companies be involved? If so, how? What would the role of the army be? It is perhaps not so far fetched: a few months before the conference, the black rat, one of the main conduits of the Black Death, reappeared in England for the first time in two hundred years.

As this book was being written, the plague broke out in Zambia in March 2001; the most recent fatality in the USA occurred in July 2001; and the UK experienced outbreaks of supposedly extinct diseases – foot & mouth and TB. Some countries, e.g. Brazil, report new cases of plague every year.

The vials containing the Seven Last Plagues from the Book of Revelation may still be waiting to be opened.

Selective Chronology of Plague Outbreaks

Earlier than 2000 BC? – the Biblical plagues recorded in Exodus and 1 Samuel.

430 B.C. The Great Plague of Athens was described by Thucydides, who survived an attack himself. The symptoms described have been variously interpreted as smallpox, typhus, bubonic plague, or most recently, Ebola. The outbreak seriously impaired the Athenian army, and prolonged the Peloponnesian War.

1st century A.D. The earliest unequivocal epidemic of bubonic plague in the Mediterranean occurred in Libya, Egypt and Syria. Described by Rufus of Ephesus, although he may not have got his information first hand.

542 The Plague of Justinian, the first pandemic of bubonic plague. About 300,000 people died in Constantinople alone during the first year. The Byzantine emperor Justinian was stricken, but recovered. However the disease crushed his ambitions to recover the full extent of the old Roman empire. Merchant ships carried the disease into the rest of the Mediterranean, and it flared up repeatedly for the next 150 years.

590 A.D. Bubonic plague killed Pope Pelagius II, who was succeeded by the reformer Gregory the Great.

627 AD The Plague of Shirawayh – the first plague of the Muslim era. This, and subsequent outbreaks in the Middle East, were part of the first pandemic.

634 AD The Plague of Yezdigird, which may be another name for...

638 AD The Plague of Amwas, which killed an entire Arab army, along with a number of the Prophet's companions.

664 AD The Plague of Cadwallader, the name for the first pandemic when it reached the British Isles.

680 A.D. Plague again struck Rome and Italy, and is credited with the origin of the cult of St. Sebastian, a third century martyr who was regarded as a protector against disease, because the epidemic abated after his bones were moved from Rome to the church of San Pietro in Vincoli in Pavia.

688 AD The Violent Plague, which swept through Basrah 'like a flood'.

706 AD The Plague of the Maidens, again in Basrah.

716 AD The Plague of the Notables, which struck Iraq and Syria.

746-748 A.D. Constantinople was struck again by plague.

1056 Plague (possibly pneumonic) in Samarkand and Balkh.

1063 An epidemic, possibly plague, hit Egypt.

1076 Epidemic of uncertain provenance in Syria.

1143 Epidemic of uncertain provenance in Syria (again) which also spread to Egypt

1148. An epidemic of uncertain provenance hit Adalia on the coast of Anatolia, which wiped out soldiers and pilgrims of the Second Crusade and facilitated their defeat by the Turks.

1157 Plague in Yemen.

1163 Yet more disease in Syria, possibly plague.

1167 The army of Frederick Barbarossa nearly destroyed by plague after successfully taking Rome.

1200 Possible outbreak in Egypt.

1217 A letter from the Jewish quarter of Old Cairo mentions an outbreak of plague.

1230 The plague recurs at Rome.

1244 The plague attacks Florence.

1258 Syria again. This time it *is* plague. (Probably)

1273 Egypt.

1284 The legendary rat-related depopulation of Hameln, in central Germany. Did the children have the plague? Was the figure of the Pied Piper a personification of natural forces? Other theories hold that they participated in the Children's Crusade (long past); that they suffered from an outbreak of Huntington's Chorea (which would account for the 'dancing' as the children were led away); that the children symbolised the young men killed at the battle of Sedemuender in 1260; that they fell into a river en masse as a bridge collapsed; or that they went to live in Bohemia, Transylvania or Berlin.

1295 Egypt again.

1320 The south of France and Spain. Jews and lepers were accused of spreading the plague by poisoning wells, and were burnt.

1333 Ditto.

1328-1351 The Black Death.

1361/62 The Children's Plague aka The Grey Death. Although not as severe as 1348/49, this was nearly as catastrophic, as it was striking a society greatly weakened and still in shock from the first outbreak. The great storm of the 15 January 1362 was widely considered a harbinger of disaster. Edward III lost two more daughters when Princesses Margaret and Mary succumbed to the plague. The *Continuation of the Polychronicon of Ralph Higden* notes that the second pestilence also affected men more than women: 'Their widows... took as their husbands foreigners and other imbeciles.' John of Reading adds that they 'shamelessly gave birth to bastards.'

1369-71 The third pestilence, according to the *Anonimalle Chronicale*, 'was great beyond measure, lasted a long time and was particularly fatal to children.'

1375 The fourth pestilence. Thomas Walsingham, in his *Historia Anglicana*, notes that 'infinite numbers of men and women were devoured by sudden death.' He also notes that the Scots were strangely immune and, 'showing themselves to be enemies of humanity', used this to their advantage in pillaging the affected English.

1390 Walsingham describes the fifth pestilence as being 'thought as bad as the great pestilence [the black death].' He believes that 11,000 people died in York 'in a short space of time.'

1405 The sixth pestilence.

1499 Plague struck again in London, causing thousands of deaths. Chroniclers had by now given up trying to number the outbreaks.

1563 Plague struck again in London, probably its worst outbreak ever, killing an estimated quarter to a third of the population. Subsequent outbreaks occurred in 1578, 1593, 1603, 1625, 1636, and 1665, each time killing thousands. In terms of proportion of the total population destroyed, the 1563 and 1665 epidemics were the worst.

1590-1610 Plague swept many European cities again. The distinctive 'bird-mask' cloaks worn by doctors date from around this time. Their robes were lined with wax, which was thought to afford protection from the plague, while the mask featured a prominent beak, which was filled with aromatic herbs.

1618-48 The period of the Thirty Years War in Germany was marked by repeated epidemics, including typhus, plague and dysentery that spread to other European countries. Its plague victims included Gustavus Adolphus, King of Sweden, and the deposed Frederick, Elector Palatine.

1625-40 Bubonic plague spread through France. Probably the worst single outbreak was in Lyon in 1628.

1665 The Great Plague. London lost at least 20 percent of its population, perhaps as many as 100,000 people. Samuel Pepys sees houses whose doors are daubed with red crosses in a deserted Drury Lane, together with the words 'Lord Have Mercy Upon Us.' The alchemist George Starkey valiantly tries to find a cure for plague, but dies after performing a post mortem on a plague victim. In Lincolnshire, Isaac Newton retires to the seclusion of his estates, where he takes the first step in formulating the theory of gravitation.

1679 Plague spreads from the Ottoman Empire into Austria, killing thousands of people especially in Vienna.

1720 Another outbreak of plague in France, centered on Marseilles, killing probably a third to half the population.

1890s The third plague pandemic began in China in the 1850s and spread slowly until it reached the seaports in the 1890s, then spread more rapidly around the world, striking particularly hard in India, Egypt and North Africa, and South America. The continental U.S. was largely spared, but Hawaii suffered a severe outbreak in 1899, and San Francisco was affected in 1900-1904, and again in 1907-1909. The second outbreak there was exacerbated by unsanitary conditions following the earthquake of 1906. Sporadic outbreaks continued worldwide for years, and officially this pandemic was not considered over until 1959. (Some argue that the third pandemic is still ongoing.)

1899-1901 The third pandemic hits Britain, with numerous outbreaks mainly in ports, such as Glasgow, Cardiff, Liverpool, Hull and London.

1910 The plague in Suffolk

1918 The plague returns to Suffolk, killing two people in June.

1921 The Manchurian epidemic. Average life expectancy of pneumonic plague victims is only 1.8 days.

1952 In one of the Cold War's more bizarre episodes, the Americans release plague-infested voles into China.

1967 Outbreaks of plague during the Vietnam war, mainly affecting the indigenous population.

1994 The plague resurfaces in India.
1997 Plague hits Mozambique and Malawi.
1998 Plague in Uganda.
1999 Malawi is infected again, as is Namibia.
2001 Plague in Zambia.

This list is still growing. To find out where plague is currently raging, see Outbreak News on the World Health Organisation website: http://www.who.int/disease-outbreak-news.

Suggestions for Further Reading

Ole Jørgen Benedictow *Plague in Late Medieval Nordic Countries* Oslo: Middelalderforlaget 1992. Benedictow concentrates mainly on the best documented of the Scandinavian countries, Norway, in addition to including one of the few in-depth studies of the plague in Iceland (not affected until 1402).

Michael W. Dols *The Black Death in the Middle East* Princeton 1977. One of the few books on the non-European plague, Dols focuses mainly on Egypt and Syria, which have the best records.

Robert Gottfried *The Black Death: Natural and Human Disaster in Medieval Europe* The Free Press 1983. A good general survey of the plague.

David Herlihy *The Black Death and the Transformation of the West* Harvard 1997. Lectures delivered by Herlihy in 1985 on the importance of the plague in forging early modern Europe.

Rosemary Horrox (Translator and Editor) *The Black Death* Manchester University Press 1994. A collection of 14th century eyewitness accounts of the plague in Europe.

Mavis E. Mate *Daughters, Wives and Widows After the Black Death* Boydell 1998. A study of the position of women after the plague, using case studies of women living in Sussex between 1350 and 1535.

Mark Ormrod & Phillip Lindley (Editors*)* *The Black Death in England* Paul Watkins 1996. A collection of four recent essays on various aspects of the plague in England.

Colin Platt *King Death* UCL Press 1996. The after-effects of the plague in England.

Graham Twigg *The Black Death: A Biological Reappraisal* Batsford Academic & Educational 1984. An overview of the pandemic, arguing that the Black Death was not exclusively bubonic plague, but was probably assisted in its work by some form of cattle disease such as anthrax. Also contains a chapter on 20th century outbreaks in the UK, including the 1910 Suffolk epidemic.

Philip Ziegler *The Black Death* Penguin 1969; Illustrated Edition Alan Sutton 1997. Still the best general account of the pestilence. The second edition includes a chapter (not by Ziegler) of the current [1998] state of Black Death research.

Related Interest

Giovanni Boccaccio *The Decameron* OUP and Penguin Classics. The references to the plague mainly occur in the introduction. This is perhaps the best known contemporary account of the Black Death.

Bruce M. S. Campbell (Editor) *Before the Black Death: Studies in the 'Crisis' of the Early Fourteenth Century* Manchester University Press 1991. A look at conditions in Europe prior to 1347.

Albert Camus *The Plague* (1947) Penguin Classics. Camus's classic novel about the plague hitting a North African town during the Second World War.

Norman F. Cantor *The Sacred Chain: A History of the Jews* Fontana 1996. Details the persecution of the Jews during the Black Death.

Daniel Defoe *A Journal of the Plague Year* (1722) OUP and Penguin Classics. The classic fictionalised account of the Great Plague of 1665. It is not an eyewitness account. Defoe based it on contemporary reports since he himself was a child at the time.

John Evelyn *The Diary of John Evelyn* Routledge/Thoemmes Press 1996. Like Pepys, Evelyn witnessed the plague in London in the summer and autumn of 1665.

Hermann Hesse *Narcissus and Goldmund* (1930). Hesse's novel about an itinerant monk has the plague as a backdrop.

George Huppert *After the Black Death: A Social History of Early Modern Europe* Indiana University Press 1998.

William H. McNeill *Plagues and Peoples* Anchor Press 1998. A general look at the social history of pandemics.

Samuel Pepys *The Diary of Samuel Pepys* Penguin Classics. Unlike Defoe, Pepys witnessed the Great Plague at first hand.

Stephen Porter *The Great Plague* Alan Sutton 1999. A study of the Great Plague of 1665. Illustrated.

Books for Children

Sarah Blackmore *The Black Death* Hodder and Stoughton 2000

Herbie Brennan *A Story about the Great Plague – Jennet's Tale* Mammoth 2000

Leonard W. Cowie *The Black Death & The Peasants' Revolt* Wayland 1986

James Day *The Black Death* Wayland 1989

Chris Jordan & Tim Wood *The Black Death: History Action Pack* Edward Arnold 1982

Tony D. Triggs The Black Death & the Peasants' Revolt Macmillan 1985

Derek Turner *The Black Death: Illustrated from Contemporary Sources* Longman 1978; 2nd edition 1988

Film

Panic in the Streets (Elia Kazan 1950) Elia Kazan's film noir stars Richard Widmark as a US Public Health Doctor in New Orleans trying to trace a killer (Jack Palance) who has contracted pneumonic plague.

The Seventh Seal (Ingmar Bergman 1957) Bergman's classic starring Max von Sydow has the plague in Sweden as a backdrop, and includes perhaps the most famous contemporary Danse Macabre, with Death leading his hapless victims over a hilltop at sunset. Apparently this was a last minute decision, shot in one take with the last of the day's film in the camera.

The Decameron (Pier Paolo Pasolini 1970) Pasolini's celebrated film version Boccaccio.

Epidemic (Lars von Trier 1987) Von Trier stars as a doctor unwittingly spreading an unknown disease in his study of the outbreak of a nameless epidemic.

The Navigator (Vincent Ward 1988) Much praised film from New Zealand, in which a team of Cumbrian villagers embark upon a quest to save their village from the plague, ending up in 20th century Auckland.

The Essential Library: Currently Available

Film Directors:

Woody Allen (Revised) (£3.99)   Tim Burton (£3.99)
Jane Campion (£2.99)   John Carpenter (£3.99)
Jackie Chan (£2.99)   Joel & Ethan Coen (£3.99)
David Cronenberg (£3.99)   Terry Gilliam (£2.99)
Alfred Hitchcock (£3.99)   Krzysztof Kieslowski (£2.99)
Stanley Kubrick (£2.99)   Sergio Leone (£3.99)
David Lynch (£3.99)   Brian De Palma (£2.99)
Sam Peckinpah (£2.99)   Ridley Scott (£3.99)
Orson Welles (£2.99)   Billy Wilder (£3.99)
Steven Spielberg (£3.99)   Mike Hodges (£3.99)
Ang Lee (£3.99)

Film Genres:

Film Noir (£3.99)   Hong Kong Heroic Bloodshed (£2.99)
Horror Films (£3.99)   Slasher Movies (£3.99)
Spaghetti Westerns (£3.99)   Vampire Films (£2.99)
Blaxploitation Films (£3.99)   Bollywood (£3.99)
French New Wave (£3.99)

Film Subjects:

Laurel & Hardy (£3.99)   Marx Brothers (£3.99)
Steve McQueen (£2.99)   Marilyn Monroe (£3.99)
The Oscars® (£3.99)   Filming On A Microbudget (£3.99)
Bruce Lee (£3.99)   Film Music (£3.99)

TV:

Doctor Who (£3.99)

Literature:

Cyberpunk (£3.99)   Philip K Dick (£3.99)
Agatha Christie (£3.99)   Noir Fiction (£2.99)
Terry Pratchett (£3.99)   Sherlock Holmes (£3.99)
Hitchhiker's Guide (Revised) (£3.99)

Ideas:

Conspiracy Theories (£3.99)   Nietzsche (£3.99)
Feminism (£3.99)

History:

Alchemy & Alchemists (£3.99)   The Crusades (£3.99)
American Civl War (£3.99)   American Indian Wars (£3.99)
Black Death (£3.99)

Available at all good bookstores, or send a cheque to: **Pocket Essentials (Dept BD), 18 Coleswood Rd, Harpenden, Herts, AL5 1EQ, UK**. Please make cheques payable to 'Oldcastle Books.' Add 50p postage & packing for each book in the UK and £1 elsewhere.